FORGOTTEN
Many times the Past holds Strength for the Present

Salvations & Martyrs

By Ronnie Brown

Copyright © 2018 by Ronnie E Brown

No part of this publication may be reproduced, distributed, or transmitted in any form or by any means, including photocopying, recording, or other electronic or mechanical methods, without the prior written permission of the author, except in the case of brief quotations embodied in critical reviews and certain other noncommercial uses permitted by copyright law. For permission requests, write to the author at the address below.

Ronnie Brown
89 Connecticut Ave
Trenton, Georgia 30752

Printed in the United States of America

First Printing, 2018

For more information on the author go to:
www.RonnieBrown.net

Dedication
To my loving wife, Carey Lynn Brown, for her patience and encouragement.

CONTENTS

INTRODUCTION 3

SALVATIONS 7

    JERRY MCAULEY 9

    MEL TROTTER 25

    ANDRES OF THE MUINANE TRIBE 37

    GENESIUS OF ROME 45

    STUART HAMBLEN 53

    CHARLOTTE ELLIOTT 59

    THE BIBLE ON THE BOUNTY 69

    THE KING OF CHATTANOOGA 81

MARTYRS 87

    WILLIAM HUNTER 89

    JOHN BROWN OF PRIESTHILL 95

    DR. ROWLAND TAYLOR 105

    MARGARET WILSON 115

    JAMES ABBES 123

MAEYKEN WENS 129

MARINUS OF CAESAREA 139

THE DEATH OF WILLIAM TYNDALE 145

THE GODLY WOMAN OF CHIPPING SODBURY 153

WATCHMAN NEE 159

EXTRAS 167

THE RED RIVER MEETING HOUSE 169

IRA SANKEY AND THE CONFEDERATE SOLDIER 179

EPILOGUE... 191

THE GOSPEL 193

SOURCES... 197

INTRODUCTION

I love the Bible. I love the divinely inspired and historical accounts of both the Old Testament and the New Testament. The stories of the lives of Moses and Malachi; of Rebecca and Ruth; of Peter and Paul; of John and above all Jesus, thrill my heart and help me to have faith in the God of the Bible.

Down through my life as a regular church attendee, when pastors and teachers have taught me the Bible, they have also interspersed stories from church history that parallel much of the truth of God found in the Scriptures. These have always fascinated me. They have shown me that the works of the eternal God are not confined to the days of antiquity. God is just as much God today as He was in the Bible.

In my late twenties, I hung on every word of my pastor, Dr. Ken Trivette, as he told of the stories of George Muller's faith in God to daily feed hundreds of orphans or the evangelistic heart of Hudson Taylor to reach the Chinese people with the gospel of Jesus Christ.

Even in children's church, when I would play guitar and sing for the kids, I secretly couldn't wait for Sister Kathy Groves to tell the missionary stories of St. Patrick or Adoniram Judson. I would sit wide-eyed with the kids to hear of how God used ordinary people to do great things.

During my seventeen years of preaching ministry (ten of which were as a pastor), I have come across countless amazing stories of God's faithfulness and ability buried in dusty books and out of the way places. Using them here and there in thousands of messages, I have called people to come to faith in Jesus Christ and to trust God in their daily life as a believer.

In 2016, while listening to a highly rated secular podcast, I realized just how effective storytelling through digital audio could be. Other similar podcasts were being downloaded by the millions. I had little doubt that there was a great hunger among millennials for narrative, for history, and for a good yarn.

A realization came into my mind, "I have a story to tell. I know stories from church history that can make people's hair stand on end. And these are stories with a redeeming value; stories of God's power and Christ's love! These stories coupled with a good Bible application could go a long way in reaching a generation for Jesus Christ." And just like that, the Forgotten Podcast was born.

Forgotten is a brief audio journey through the historical happenings of the Christian faith. Each episode recounts the acts of God's supernatural Hand in the events of man or contains the testimony of extraordinary sacrifice by devoted followers of Jesus Christ. My heart's desire for the podcast is to share to as many people as possible the saving life of God's Son, Jesus Christ. And to also strengthen the faith of God's people in God and compel them to resolve their hearts to trust Him no matter what. The reason for telling these stories is that we may not forget. Let us never be accused of forgetting our God like the people of the Prophet Jeremiah's day, where God said, "…yet my people have forgotten me…" (Jeremiah 2:32)

The following chapters represent the transcripts of several episodes of the Forgotten Podcast that focus on two subjects:

Salvations and Martyrdoms. The salvation stories are of individuals from all walks of life and in different periods of world history. In each case, these stories stand as a testimony of God's power to change the hearts and lives of people who put their faith in Jesus Christ.

As Paul said in 1 Timothy 1:15 "This is a faithful saying, and worthy of all acceptation, that Christ Jesus came into the world to save sinners; of whom I am chief." Paul describes himself as the chief of sinners, as the worst of the worst, as if to say, "If God can save me, He can save you!" These stories follow in that same tradition. Just think of them as a handful of people in a long line of miracles.

The second section tells the stories of martyrs; those who have paid the ultimate price for their faith in Jesus Christ. There is something about such accounts that commands the attention of the Christian. The truth is that very few, if any, reading this book will pay such a price, but it does challenge our faith and calls us to recognize the preciousness of the gospel of Jesus Christ.

Those that have opposed the gospel of grace down through history have reckoned that the most intimidating punishment they could inflict upon believers was to torture and kill them. But this has the opposite effect. Early Christian author and apologist, Tertullian, had it right when he wrote: "The blood of the martyrs is the seed of the church."

This is still true today. Recounting these stories that have faded from the collective consciousness of the church, drive us to our knees with thankful hearts for the high price that others have paid for the faith we continue to enjoy; and cause us to stand with boldness in the face of our own opposition.

I hope this first volume of Forgotten Podcast episodes is a blessing to the hearts of individuals around the world. But most importantly, my prayer is that these accounts from history will point people to the Bible, and there discover the word of God's one theme, its one focus, the one hope of all humanity: The Son of God, Jesus Christ.

- Ronnie Brown
Trenton, Georgia
October, 2018

SALVATIONS

JERRY McAULEY

In the close confines of the urban jungle, they are not hard to find. Some of them are more forward than others not really caring if you see them or not. But most try to stay hidden. People hurriedly making their way down the city streets pretend like they are not there. Treating them like some family ghost, which if they ignored long enough, will just quietly go away.

But these people are no ghosts. They may be people who are haunted by the incessant and gnawing bite of addiction, but they're not ghosts. They may be people who are trapped in the nightmare of mental or emotional abnormality, but they're not apparitions. They may be people who, through a series of life-altering catastrophes, have seen their world come crumbling down around them, but they're not phantoms.

No, they are very much flesh and bone. Those yellow bloodshot eyes are not that much different from yours. In the right conditions of summer's heat or winter's chill, the skin that covers your hand would look just as dry and leathery as theirs.

Jerry was one of those back alley homeless and nameless people that shop owners and townsfolk wish would vanish into thin air. He was a misfit, a thief and an all-around menace to society. One might think that seven years in the state penitentiary and a good dose of jailhouse religion would have gone a long way in changing Jerry. But it didn't. Once a free man, he hit the streets again, this time plunging in deeper and deeper into wickedness; thinking that somehow he had outstretched the bounds of the love of God.

But at the last, God was there with an extended hand of love each time he fell. Until one day, it was he that God was using as His extended hand of love and compassion to the fallen. A helping hand that reached out to thousands languishing on the streets of New York City with a hot meal, a clean bed, and the life-changing message of Jesus Christ. And it was he who sparked a movement that for the last 140 years has impacted the lives of millions of people.

- ಸಿಂಡ -

Jerry McAuley was born in Ireland in 1839. From the moment of his birth, it seemed the deck was stacked against him. His family disintegrated not long after he entered this world. His father was a criminal, a counterfeiter by trade and had forsaken his family to run from the law. Not much is known of his mother. Either she could not or would not care for this child and gave him over to his grandmother.

JERRY MCAULEY

This woman was little more than a guardian on paper. Young Jerry was never sent to school; was never taught to read; he was allowed to practically come and go as he pleased which led to constant run-ins with the authorities. On top of this, no matter into whose hands he was entrusted, he suffered abuse and harsh treatment.

Finally at the age of 13, in exasperation, Jerry's grandmother sent him to the United States to live with his sister in New York City. Although he started out with legitimate employment, working for his brother-in-law, he quickly began to stoop down into a life of dishonesty and theft. Before long, Jerry was out of his sister's home and living by his wits on the streets. He would work for what he could and then steal the rest.

After a while, he came into possession of a boat that he would use to steal cargo from docked ships in the New York harbor under the cloak of darkness. He and a few cohorts would wade into the waters by night, thieving all that they could, then by day, sell their goods, and then paint the town red. He became a notorious nuisance to the 4th ward in lower Manhattan.

Although what Jerry McAuley had in fact done as a river thief was enough to send him to prison a hundred times over, the charges that caught up to him were, by his own account, entirely not of his doing. He was charged with highway robbery. Local merchants and store owners saw a chance to rid themselves of the young man. So they pointed the finger at Jerry for the crime. Without much of any legal defense, McAuley was sentenced to fifteen years hard labor in the state-prison known as Sing-Sing.

FORGOTTEN

Even though untaught to read, he had picked up some sounds and letters along the way, enough to be able to read the haunting words above the entrance to the prison: "...the way of transgressors is hard." (Proverbs 13:15) This was a phrase that was often repeated and familiar to those who made a life of sin and lawlessness even though it is a verse from the Bible. To Jerry, the path his life had taken him was hard. He wanted to die. Fifteen years in the infamous Sing-Sing Prison, for a crime he didn't commit? Sure he had done a lot that merited a stiff penalty, but to know that he was in prison, doing time for someone who walked away scot-free; the thought of someone happily walking at liberty while he suffered for their wrong, threw him into a rage and then sank him into depression.

At length, he thought it best not to fight against the prison environment, but to attempt to follow its rules in hopes that, by some means, his sentence might be cut short. But this was not easy to do in 19th-century Sing-Sing. The prisoners were held to a strict silent system. Prisoners ate in silence. They worked in silence. They existed in a world of unbroken hush.

When that silence was violated, there were harsh consequences. There were water tortures, where water was allowed to drip on an inmate's head from a high distance for hours at a time. Others included solitary confinement; flogging with whips; and bucking, which was hanging a man upside down for long periods of time.

Each time Jerry slipped up, each time he was punished, it only made him harder and harder. After five years at Sing-Sing, Jerry was miserable. He had poured himself into learning to read and write with some measure of success. But what he fed his mind upon only fueled a murderous hatred for the ones who landed him in jail.

One particular Sunday, he chose to go with the majority of men to the chapel service rather than languish with despair in his cell. As he entered the room, his eyes fixed upon a familiar face on the platform. In his former days, running the streets, Jerry did some prize fighting. Orville Gardner was a fighter, a gambler, and an all-around thug. Known as Awful Gardner, he was a brutal boxer, touted as one of the best fighting men in New York, he was favored to defeat Dominick Bradley for the Heavyweight Championship of America. But after serving a stint in Sing-Sing himself, Gardner was converted in the 1857 New York City revival. One might see him as America's first celebrity convert to Christianity. He became a powerful preacher.

When Jerry McAuley saw him that day, he remembered him as a callused criminal. You can imagine the shock that came upon Jerry when Gardner began to speak. Gardner said he was uncomfortable standing behind the pulpit, thinking himself unworthy to speak from such a place. He came down to the floor level among the men, and there gave a tear-filled testimony of how he had been where they were sitting only a few years ago.

He told them of the life-changing power of Jesus Christ and how God had worked in his life. It wasn't long before he knelt down and through his sobs asked God to do a work in the hearts of the men in that room. There was not a dry eye in the place. Jerry was doing everything that he could to hold back the tears for fear of what others would think. Jerry knew Orville. He knew that God had worked a genuine miracle in this man's life

FORGOTTEN

During his plea, Gardner mentioned a verse from the Bible which had a profound impact upon McAuley's heart. He never knew that the old book, which he thought was only for priests and saints, could speak so powerfully, revealing his own heart. He determined to find the verse that Gardner quoted.

When he returned to his cell, he took out the Bible given to him when he entered the prison, dusted it off and opened it. "Where do I go to find those words?" he asked himself. He thought he must start at the beginning and read it through. Although the verse that ignited his search was soon forgotten, another fire began to burn in his heart. He could not put the Bible down. Every day he poured over its pages, drinking in its truth. As soon as his work shift was complete, he hurried to his cell and read until the wee hours of the morning.

One night, while turning all that he had read over in his mind, and the change that had been made in the life of Gardner, he had a burning desire to have that same transformation. "What should I do?" he thought. Something seemed to tell him that he ought to pray. But what should he pray? His mind was drawn to the prayer of the publican, "God be merciful to me a sinner." He knew that he should call upon God, but he was ashamed to kneel down before God. He would fall upon his knees, but then immediately, out of embarrassment, stand up again.

The word "Whosoever" rang in his ears. "That's me." He would say. "But I'm so wicked, everything but a murderer, and that many a time in my will." But with every objection, the words of scripture he had read came to the surface of his mind. This conflict went on for weeks. He would try to pray, then would rise unable to call on God; wondering if, by his wavering heart, he would exhaust the longsuffering of God.

Finally one night, he resolved to stay on his knees until forgiveness of sin was found. On those cold stones, with clasped hands, he would pray, and then he would stop, and then he would pray again, then stop. He became desperate, assuring himself that if he did not find relief this night, he would never pray again. As he persisted in seeking God, something happened.

McAuley, in his own words, said of the experience, "All at once it seemed as if something supernatural was in my room. I was afraid to open my eyes. I was in agony, and the sweat rolled off my face in great drops. Oh, how I longed for God's mercy! Just then, in the very height of my distress, it seemed as if a hand was laid upon my head, and these words came to me: 'My son, thy sins, which are many, are forgiven.' I do not know if I heard a voice, yet the words were distinctly spoken. Oh, the precious Christ! How plainly I saw him, lifted on the cross for my sins! What a thrill went through me. I jumped from my knees; I paced up and down my cell. A heavenly light seemed to fill it; a softness and perfume like the fragrance of sweetest flowers. I did not know if I was living or not. I clapped my hands and shouted, 'Praise God! Praise God!'"

The transformation that he had first witnessed in the heart of Orville Gardner had come to reside in his own heart. He was a changed man. The heavyweight of vengeance and resentment for his being sent to prison had evaporated like the dew in the noonday summer sun. The prison walls became a sanctuary, and his labor became a delight. The ridicule and sneers of other inmates that used to be a constant fear were nothing compared to the joy of knowing and walking with Jesus. His heart erupted with love and thanksgiving to God for what he had done in his life. He became a witness to all the other men that he had the chance to encounter. God began to do a great work from cell to cell through Jerry McAuley, and many started to read their Bibles, to call upon God, and to worship Jesus in the days to follow.

For the next two years, Jerry grew in the Lord and encouraged other men in their walk with Jesus. He lived a simple life of faith. There was nothing which Jerry would encounter that could not be overcome by the power of Christ in his life. After a while, although with some hesitation, he began to pray to God that he would be set free from the prison. And sure enough, it wasn't long that he received a pardon from the governor and after having served only half of his sentence, he was released from prison.

Upon his release, he purposed to stay clear of old acquaintances from the Fourth Ward and to find a prayer meeting. He did find one, but while pacing outside for a while decided not to go into the place. He had never been to a house of worship on the outside of the prison walls, and after no one invited him in to join them, he left in frustration.

Soon, out of necessity, he enquired of an old friend where he might find a place to stay. His friend directed him to a room above a saloon. This friend soon entreated him to join him in a new drink that had become popular while Jerry was in prison. He said it was harmless, as harmless as root beer. It was a Lager beer. Jerry reluctantly agreed, and with one glass, an old appetite was awakened within him; and it wasn't long before he was drinking it every day.

JERRY MCAULEY

Thus began a spiral away from God, and the commitments that he had made upon his exit from prison. He went from small job to small job, each one being shadier than the last. Eventually, he began working back on the river, buying and selling stolen and smuggled goods, trading in counterfeit money, even thieving along the riverboats at night.

This was not all done without one objection of conscience. Jerry could not escape the memory of what he experienced in prison, the thrill of sins forgiven, the joy of winning others to Jesus, and the peace of living in the will of God. This was all brought into sharp focus one night while on the river.

He and a few others were out looking for what they could steal, and they latched on to a ferry boat to pull them back across the river to New York. At mid-river, an alarm sounded. The ferry was on fire, and it was spreading quickly. He and his friends tried to separate themselves from the ship, but two men leaped from the deck to get onto the small boat. Jerry and his partners quickly rowed them to shore and then set back out, not to save others, but to see what they could steal from the distressed vessel.

Upon arriving back at the burning ferry, several more desperate passengers saw them and leaped toward them for safety. Grudgingly, the men took as many as possible on to the boat while others clung to its sides. The whole scene with the fire, the screams, and the desperation, called to Jerry's mind the vivid scenes of hell from the Bible, the final destiny of the sinner.

On another occasion, while trying to steal from a boat on the river, the Captain was awakened by their attempt and fired his revolver at them as many as four times. Jerry could hear the daggers of hot lead whizz past his ears. Although he and his partners escaped unharmed, the thought of one of those bullets splitting his skull caused him to think over and over, "What if that bullet had hit me? What would become of me? Where would I be?" Jerry knew that the path he was on was wrong, and yet he could not stop. His only cure for the nagging reminders of God was to drown each of them in whiskey.

One night, Jerry and his partner were on the river near Brooklyn looking for what they could steal. Jerry was so intoxicated that when they did find something they could plunder, he was of no use and was left in the boat to sleep it off. Later, by some mishap, Jerry fell into the water and was helpless to save himself. As he tried, the vessel simply floated away. The river weighted him down until Jerry finally sunk beneath it. He touched the bottom of the shallow river bed and pushed himself back up. Then it all happened again. Finally, he knew that this was the last time. It seemed as though hell opened up beneath him.

Then the thought came into his mind, "Call on God." He recoiled at the idea at first, after all, he had done, how could he call on God? But the fear of death overpowered his reluctance; he cried out to God for help. Miraculously, the boat that had drifted away from him suddenly drew to within his grasp and somehow he was able to climb back on board. While heaving for breaths, a clear impression was made in his heart: This was the last time. Jerry tried to drink and drink to drive this impression from his mind, but the convicting power of God would not release his mind.

Jerry tried to find some means of legitimate employment, but could not hold down a job because of his addiction to the bottle. One day, while sitting in a room, no doubt from which he would be evicted in coming days, Jerry heard a man ask someone nearby, "Do you love Jesus?" These words arrested his attention because they sounded so much like the words he used back in Sing-Sing so long ago. He listened for and watched the man until he finally got up the courage to talk to him.

The young man was a missionary from the Howard Mission station in New Bowery. It was a place that did all that it could to help the down and outers on the street. When Jerry arrived, they asked him to sign a pledge not to drink, not to be involved in crime, and in return, they would attempt to find him employment. Jerry signed the agreement, figuring that he had nothing to lose. But he also warned the men that he probably would not be able to keep it. The men's response was only for him to try.

Hours later, back with his riverboat partner, he took a glass of whiskey in his hand pledging that this would be the last. His friend joked, "Yeah, until the next!" Suddenly the missionary walked into the room. McAuley, surprised by his appearance, did all that he could to avoid him. The minister invited Jerry on a walk.

During the walk, Jerry confided to the missionary that he was going to go out on the river that night to steal what he could. He had no choice, he was dead broke, and he had to eat. The missionary looked at Jerry and said, "Before you do that, I'll take this coat off my back and pawn it, and give you the money." Jerry saw that the coat was old and tattered. Truth be known, this man did not have much more money than him. Jerry hung his head in shame as tears trickled down his cheeks. The missionary asked Jerry to live by the word of Jesus, "Seek ye first the kingdom of

God, and his righteousness; and all these things shall be added unto you." Jerry said he would, he would trust God. The missionary then went away and in a few hours came back with 50 cents. It was enough to get something to eat and prevent him from going out to steal that night.

That missionary was a true friend to Jerry, and before long, God was once again dealing with this prodigal's heart. One night, this friend invited Jerry into his home for dinner. After the meal, as the family was singing, Jerry began to be sorrowful, weeping over all that had happened in his life. He asked the missionary to pray for him. In response, the minister encouraged him to call out to God himself. Jerry replied, "I don't know how. I can't put the words together." "Pray to God the prayer of the publican: God be merciful to me a sinner." replied the missionary. Jerry prayed it over and over again. Then the missionary said, "Put in, 'For Jesus sake.'"

There was something about that moment that was breaking for Jerry McAuley. He was given a genuine assurance of the saving power of Jesus. Joy once again filled his heart and life. A joy that had been exiled from his soul for years. Oh the mercy and grace of a God that would not give up on such a hardened, wretched, and wayward son.

This missionary friend would see Jerry through a few more times of faltering, but nowhere near the extent of what he went through after leaving Sing-Sing. This was because he had a Christian brother to help him up, to pray for him, and keep him accountable. Jerry was able to find steady work for a time. And when the work ran out, he was strong enough in the Lord to go into his closet and ask God to meet his need instead of wading into a river of crime.

During one day at work, Jerry had somewhat of a vision. He described it in these words, "I was singing at my work, and my mind became absorbed, and it seemed as if I was working for the Lord down in the Fourth Ward. I had a house, and people were coming in. There was a bath, and as they came in I washed and cleansed them outside, and the Lord cleansed them inside. They came at the first by small numbers, then by hundreds, and afterward by thousands." From somewhere within his heart, he was asked, "Would you do that for the Lord if he should call you? Would you do it for Jesus' sake?" Jerry's answer was, "Yes, Lord, open the way, and I will go."

This vision burned in his heart. And he begged God for the opportunity to share it with others. On two different occasions, God did open the door to share his vision with Christians gathered at special meetings. Several sums of money were donated to the project. Altogether, he was given $450 toward the work.

There was a house down in the Fourth Ward that was owned by the City Mission and Tract Society. They recommended that 316 Water Street be placed at Jerry McAuley's disposal for this work. In October 1872, he took the $450 and applied it to the cleaning and repair of the building. A sign was placed out front, "Helping Hand for Men."

The Helping Hand building was renovated and prepared to be a beacon of hope for the hopeless and aimless men of the Fourth Ward. The repair was completed in November of that year. And on Thanksgiving Day in 1872, the first meal was offered to the needy there at the Helping Hand for Men at 316 Water Street. A table was spread and a number of the needy and outcast not only enjoyed a hearty meal, but they were in attendance at a worship service. A worship service where God mightily poured out his Holy Spirit and moved upon the hearts of all present. There was such a sense of the overwhelming presence of God that they decided to do the same thing again the next night, and then the next night, and then the following night.

Jerry served at the Helping Hand for the next 10 years. Scores of men were assisted and converted by the grace of God at that time. When he left in 1882, it was to start the Cremorne Mission not far from Times Square as a "beachhead in a vast jungle of vice and debauchery."

He labored there for two years before he passed away on a September afternoon in 1884. He died of tuberculosis which he had contracted while in Sing-Sing Prison years ago. Renowned poet and songwriter Fanny Crosby, who was a regular at the mission, singing, and serving, was inspired by the life of Jerry McAuley to write a prayer which later was turned into a song:

Lord, behold in Thy compassion
Those who kneel before Thee now;
They are in a sad condition
None can help them, Lord, but Thou.
They are lost but do not leave them
In their dreary path to roam;
There is pardon, precious pardon

JERRY MCAULEY

If to Thee by faith they come.

The vision that God gave Jerry McAuley was not only realized in his lifetime but can be found all across the length and breadth of the United States. In the maze of city streets, where so many are lost in ruin and addiction, chances are, that just a few blocks away, there is a Christian ministry whose calling is to take in the homeless, offer them a place to be bathed and cleansed on the outside, in hopes that Jesus would clean the inside.

So many that occupy the park benches and sidewalks of our cities are not much different than Jerry. Someone that has fallen again and again and again. So many times that those nearby may be tempted to give up on them. But God never grows weary of the clay and throws it away. His persistent love continues to reach out a helping hand to those that are broken. And it is Christians who are left with this responsibility:

> *Brethren, if a man be overtaken in a fault, ye which are spiritual, restore such an one in the spirit of meekness… (Galatians 6:1)*

MEL TROTTER

He waited until everybody was gone. His wife and her family, the pastor and scattered friends had all said their goodbyes to the lifeless body of his two-year-old son. He was able to find an unlocked door to slip into the funeral parlor. As he came into the room, the sight of the singular small white coffin against the far end of the room was chilling. Only hours ago, he stood above that coffin with his heart-broken wife and pledged that he would never do it again. But he couldn't think about that now. He had to rid himself of that sick, nauseous feeling in the pit of his stomach. His heart was racing as he felt like the weight of the world was on his chest.

He reached down and lifted the lid. There was his son; his boy. It seemed like just yesterday that he was born. He had gotten so big so fast. And now he was dead, gone forever. His cheeks were pail in the dim light of the room. As Mel reached out to touch the tender arm of his child, his hand recoiled. It was cold and hard.

FORGOTTEN

His fingers slightly twisted the dainty clothes on the child. He had never seen this outfit, before. His wife couldn't afford such clothes. Someone must have taken pity on the impoverished family and donated something for the child's burial. But instead of admiring the kindness expressed in the clothes, Mel only thought that there was no way he could take the clothes off of the child. No matter what they were worth, he just couldn't do it.

Then he saw the shoes, brand new little white shoes. Shoes that would bring at least a couple of bucks. "Does a dead child really need shoes?" he thought. Probably no one would even notice the next day. So in the shadowy dim light of the room, Mel reached a trembling hand down, down into the coffin, and slipped the tiny shoes from the body of his two-year-old son. With shoes in hand, he quickly made his way out of the parlor, down to the nearest saloon, and slapped the little shoes down on the counter and said, "Give me a drink! I'm dying for a drink!"

As the whiskey burned its way down his throat, the nauseating pain went away, the tremble in his hand subsided, and the heavy weight lifted into a dull numbing haze, at least for the next few hours.

- ᛉ)ᛟ -

Melvin Ernest Trotter was born on May 16, 1870, in Orangeville, Illinois. He was one of seven children born to an alcoholic father William and a Bible-believing mother, Emily Jane. William Trotter's trade of tending bar at a local saloon did not help his addiction to alcohol. It was said that he drank just about as much as he served. As a little boy, Mel (as he was called) learned the family trade, so that he could pour drinks when his dad was passed out on the floor.

But young Mel made up his mind that he was not going to live his life in a saloon, like his father. He was going to make something of himself. In 1877, when Mel was 17-years-old, he left home and moved to Freeport, Illinois. It was there that he became a barber and quite a good one. He earned a good living for himself; so much so that he had a little extra money which he spent many nights gambling and drinking heavily.

Although he was drunk most of the time, he was able to keep it together enough to hold down his job as a barber and also to garner the attention of a young lady by the name of Lottie. When Mel wasn't drunk, he had a contagious smile and a quick Irish wit that could woo the attention of any naive woman. He was charming and considerate when he wasn't drinking.

In 1891 Mel and Lottie were married. Everything seemed like a sweet storybook ending for Lottie until she discovered the dark secret that Mel desperately tried to keep from her while they were engaged: his drinking. By the time she realized the horrifying truth, it was too late. Mel could no longer stay sober enough to work at the barbershop. He tried selling insurance for a while, but that only lasted a few weeks.

Don't get the idea that Mel was indifferent to his behavior. He wasn't. He hated what he was doing to his wife and marriage. Each time he would go on a binge, he would come home weeping and begging his wife's forgiveness; telling her again and again that he would never drink another drop. Lottie tried to help him. She forgave him and gave him another chance time after time.

FORGOTTEN

Friends attempted to step in and help. But in each case, it was only a matter of a few days before he would be on another drunken spree.

It was about this time that Lottie gave birth to a little boy. Mel was a father now. Lottie couldn't bear the thought of life going on as usual now with a baby in the family. So, with the help of some friends, they were able to move away from the city some eleven miles. This would put them far enough away from the bars and the gambling houses that Mel could not easily go on a binge. And to Lottie's surprise, it worked! Mel stayed sober. The Trotter household started to enjoy some amount of normalcy. Mel found steady work out near the house. They were even able to afford a horse and buggy to get around. Lottie kept a close eye on her husband and prayed for him incessantly, and for all she knew, God was answering her prayers. But what she didn't realize was that the demons which haunted the heart of Mel Trotter had not vanished, but were just merely hidden.

One winter night, after visiting some friends, Ms. Trotter went inside to tuck the baby into bed. And after Mel was long in coming in from stabling the horse, she began to worry. She went outside to find the horse and buggy gone, along with her husband. All that was left were a set of wagon wheel tracks in the snow, heading toward town.

Mel arrived in town at the saloon, parked the horse and buggy out back and struck up a deal with the bartender for bar credit to the value of the rig. Mel entered the bar with a shout, "The drinks are on me! Everybody have something to drink. Drink up the horse!" Hours later he staggered his way home the eleven miles in the snow; greeting his wife with promise after promise never to touch another drop. Yet, after another commitment, and another move, and another fresh start, the drunken sprees came again and again. Now Mel was staying away from home for days at a time.

Once after a 10-day drunken fog, Mel sobered up enough to come home. He opened the door of his home to find his wife heaving with tears while she held the lifeless body of their two-year-old son in her arms. The only thought running through the heart-broken mind of Mel was "I'm a murderer!"

Later as Lottie stood with Mel over the little white coffin that held the cold body of their dead son, she once again pleaded with him to stop the madness of his drinking. She begged him to promise to her that he would never take another drink. With tears streaming down his face, and with every sincere intention from the depths of his soul he said he would never touch another drop. But only a few hours later, he slipped into the funeral parlor, took the shoes off of his dead child's feet, and gave them to the bartender for a few more glasses of whiskey.

Moments later, after the first twinges of sobriety started to sweep over his mind, Mel knew that it was over; he had sunk to the lowest of the low. He was the reason his son lay in that casket. In his mind, he was nothing more than a worthless drunken bum. It was time to put an end to his miserable life.

He somehow found his way onto an empty boxcar, and on January 19, 1897, ended up in Chicago, Ill. That sickening craving of his body for liquor had awakened over the long trip. He made his way downtown in the bitterly cold wind. Finding his way to the Clark Street saloon, he put up his own shoes, along with his

FORGOTTEN

hat, and coat for a couple more glasses of whiskey. Yet in only a few hours, he was thrown out on to the street.

He was freezing. His bare feet were stinging as he walked across the snow. Finally, the thought crossed his mind. Lake Michigan was just a few blocks away. All he could think of was jumping into that lake and ending it all; He just wanted it to be over. He couldn't take it anymore. Enough was enough.

But his path to Lake Michigan led him past old Van Buren Street, where was the Pacific Garden Mission. "The Old Lighthouse" as it is often called, was established as a homeless shelter in 1877 by Colonel George Clarke and his wife, Sarah. The building was previously known as the Pacific Beer Garden. When Colonel Clark approached Evangelist D.L. Moody as to what to name the building, he suggested that they keep the name of the former occupant and just drop the word beer. For years it had stood as a beacon of hope and help for the homeless on the streets of Chicago. About 10 years earlier a Chicago White Sox outfielder by the name of Billy Sunday had been converted in that very same mission.

That night, Tom Mackey, an ex-jockey, and former faro-dealer, himself a recent convert, was standing his post on the street in front of the mission door. It was so bitterly cold that night. No one would have argued with him if he had just stepped inside to warm up a little bit. Besides, no one in their right mind would be out in these blizzard conditions. But something within Tom kept saying, "Just wait a little longer. You may not be able to do a whole lot for the Lord, but you can wait out here and look for somebody." Sure enough, the ex-jockey, saw a staggering figure come out from the shadows. He placed his hand on his shoulder and with a few kind words just led Mel into the mission. The room was packed with men. Men with stories just like Mel's. Tom led him over to an empty chair by the chimney and leaned him up against the wall.

That night the superintendent of the Pacific Garden Mission, Harry Monroe, was leading the worship service. He had seen Tom Mackey bring the huddled man in through the mission doors, and he breathed a prayer to God, "Oh God, save that poor boy!"

Moments later, the slumbering Mel began to stir. The last thing he remembered, he was on his way to jump into Lake Michigan and now he is in a religious service. With these conscious thoughts came the memory of that little white coffin and the death of his young son. He could almost hear the pleadings of his wife again. Then something the preacher said arrested his attention: "I was twenty-seven years old when I wandered into this Mission." You see, the story of Harry Monroe was not much different than that of Mel Trotter. Helpless and penniless, he found his way into the selfsame mission years earlier.

Maybe it was the fact that Harry's story was so similar to his own. Perhaps it was the fact that Harry was now the superintendent of the mission that was once his last hope. Maybe it was merely the fact that Mel was 27 just like Harry had been when he first arrived at this place. Whatever it was, it captured the attention of Trotter. It brought a sobriety that he had not known in quite some time, and Mel hung on every word. At the close of the message, Mr. Monroe said, "Jesus loves you, and so do I, put up your hand for prayer, let God know you want to make room for Him in your heart."

FORGOTTEN

At that, Mel raised his hand, rose to his feet and fumbled forward to the altar. Harry knelt down beside him and shared the story of God's love in Jesus Christ again. How that Christ died for his sins; and that by repentance and faith in Jesus, God would forgive his sin. At that moment Mel cried out for God's mercy and forgiveness, and God reached down and took a black and dead heart of wickedness, and cleansed it with Christ's blood and made it alive! You see Mel did die that night. But not in the depths of Lake Michigan; that night the old Mel died in the depths of God's redeeming love!

That moment not only was occupied by a new saving life imparted to Mel Trotter but in that selfsame moment, the chains of addiction to alcohol were forever broken. Never again would Mel Trotter taste another drop of alcohol. In his autobiography, Trotter said of this moment, "There is no question in my mind that the greatest day I ever lived was the 19th day of January 1897, when the Lord Jesus came into my life and saved me from my sin...The old things passed away so thoroughly that I have never once wanted the things which dominated my life."

Mel Trotter slowly began to put his life back together. He started working again as a barber and spent his evenings down at the mission. It wasn't long before he sent for his wife to come and be with him there in Chicago. For the first time since she married Mel, she felt happy and secure. Mel started playing the guitar and singing songs during the worship services. It wasn't long before he and Harry Monroe were going to supporting churches and representing the mission. Whenever he had a moment, he was out and about the city streets of Chicago looking for drunks to tell them that there is hope in Jesus Christ and inviting them to believe on Jesus.

MEL TROTTER

In 1900, under the recommendation of Monroe, Mel Trotter became the director of the Grand Rapids Rescue Mission in Grand Rapids, Michigan. Located in the down and out red-light district of the city, almost immediately, people began to be saved under the ministry of Trotter. Trotter had a good business sense as well as a hardnosed determination. He preached and sang in the services, as well as handled the day to day necessities of managing such a ministry. On one occasion, he had the crowd sing "More About Jesus" while he tossed the hooligans into the street that were disturbing the service.

He also had a heart for those broken by sin. Mel led Herb Sillaway, who happened to be a drunken barber himself, to the Lord. But for Sillaway the pull of addiction did not break as readily. He fell and got drunk six times in a four week period. As a result, he tried to drown himself. Trotter found him in a jail cell wet from his suicide attempt. Mel just stood in front of him and wept like a baby. Sillaway said, "My God, man, I believe you love me." Trotter replied, "Yes, Herb, I love you like I love my own soul." Sillaway eventually became Trotter's assistant at the mission.

During his 40 years as director of the Grand Rapids Rescue Mission, he saw scores of people come to faith in Jesus Christ. He started a Mission Sunday School that had an attendance of three to five hundred children, who were often fed and clothed as well as hearing the gospel story. By 1913, the mission held twenty-three meetings a week, and the building was in constant use twenty-four hours a day providing food, clothing, and lodging. Trotter preached in prison services and held Bible classes and street meetings. He led evangelistic services among the troops during World War I. Some estimates suggest that 16,000 soldiers

FORGOTTEN

came to Christ in those meetings. He preached alongside Billy Sunday in crusades all over the country.

In a rare recording of one of his sermons, Trotter preached: "...Take it from God's book. Now I not going to sit here and try to tell you today that God keeps books like I used to think He did when I was a boy. I used to think that every good thing that I did would be put down and every bad thing I did would be put down, and then when I got ready to die they'd add up the good ones and add up the bad ones and subtract the difference and if I done more evil than good, I'd go to hell and perish. And if I did the other way, I'd go to heaven. Now I know that isn't so.

And yet, I tell you God keeps books. God knows you and God knows even the thought and intent of the heart. Now if that is so, there's nothing but eternal punishment ahead of me. You see, but there's hope. There is hope in this text: I, even I, am he that blotteth out thy transgressions for mine own sake, and will not remember thy sins. (Isaiah 43:25).

You see it's a commercial term: I'm in debt, and he paid my debt. It's a chemical term, like an ink eradicator, He blotted them out. You see judgment has gone ahead! My, my, that's a comfort to me...Thank God the whole thing has been blotted out!"

In 1939, Trotter suffered a severe heart attack in Kannapolis, North Carolina, and he later died at his summer cottage near Holland, Michigan in 1940. At his funeral, some of Trotter's close friends shared stories that reflected what kind of man he was. One recalled that he would pray with an alcoholic, "then stand him on his feet and say, 'Now go home and get the wife and kiddies and come down to the Mission tonight.' Then as they parted, Trotter would slip a dollar bill or a silver dollar in the poor drunkard's hand. I heard one of those men say, as he stood outside the Mission door, after such a parting, 'I will die before I spend this dollar on booze.'"

On January 19, 1897, Mel Trotter was looking for death; a death that would end his miserable existence. But the truth is, Mel was already dead. As far as God was concerned, he was dead; dead in his sin; dead in his rebellion; dead in his lawlessness before God. But on that January night, while he was looking for death, he found life; new life; resurrection life. The life that is found in only one place, for Jesus said,

He that heareth my word, and believeth on him that sent me, hath everlasting life, and shall not come into condemnation; but is passed from death unto life. (John 5:24)

ANDRES OF THE MUINANE TRIBE

The Gospel of Jesus Christ, the centerpiece of the Christian faith, can be easily and straightforwardly be laid out in a rather simple and understandable way: All have sinned; all people have broken God's rules. And the punishment for that sin is death, eternal separation from God in a burning hell. But God has given the gift of eternal life to mankind through His own Son Jesus, who suffered and died on the cross. And by believing on, by trusting in Jesus, our sin can be forgiven, and the gift of everlasting life can be ours to have.

The gospel of Jesus Christ is clear, comprehensive, and reasonable. It is heart compelling; showing us our need, revealing the consequences of our sin, and then presenting us with the cure: Jesus of Nazareth, the miracle worker from Galilee, one who died long ago on a Roman cross just outside the city of Jerusalem. It is the sweet story of God's redeeming love for fallen man.

FORGOTTEN

But when thinking of these truths, it does not take long for one to come to a very perplexing question: What about those that have never heard? This world has over 7.5 Billion people spread across 7 massive continents. Even though Christians have been carrying the good news of Jesus throughout the world for nearly 2000 years, there are still people groups in thick jungles and high deserts and far-reaching environments that have yet to even hear of the name of Jesus. For centuries, generations have come and gone, they have lived and died never hearing the good news of Jesus Christ. And according to the Holy Scriptures, upon their death, they enter a hopeless eternity of pain and suffering. The question is: "Is that fair?"

The Bible says that all men have the testimony of the created world and the heart conscience to expose on to the living God. They can look up into the starry heavens and know there is a God. They can probe the depths of their own heart and know that one day they will stand before God. But yet they are without that Name; that Name above all other names; that name without which no man can be saved: The name of Jesus.

The question is really this: Is God big enough to bring the name of Jesus to the heart of a man that has responded in thirst to the witness of creation and conscience, even when that man lives in the secluded isolation of a South American rainforest? The answer to this question is a resounding, "Yes!"

- ഗ)൙ -

The Muinane are an indigenous tribal people that live in the little village of La Sabana, in Amazonas, in the southernmost state of

ANDRES OF THE MUINANE TRIBE

Columbia. During the late 1800s and the beginning of the 20th century, the Muinane were mercilessly exploited during the Amazon rubber boom. For the civilized world to enjoy raincoats, automobile tires and rubber balls, these people, who were completely isolated from the civilized world, were enslaved tortured and subjected to near genocide. The inhumanity that took place incited author Richard Collier to write a book entitled "The River That God Forgot."

By 1964, the Muinane were as isolated as ever, driven further into the jungle to retreat from the "rubber hunters." They were extremely suspicious of anyone from the outside world. The Muinane were led by a capable Chief who sought to protect his people from the ravages that they had suffered in years gone by. This chief had a son in his mid-twenties by the name of Andrés. In 1964, Andrés was living about three days' journey away from his home village of La Sabana near the Caquetá River. He had become indebted to a local rubber baron for a transistor radio. Day after day, he would get up very early in the morning and make his way around to hundreds of rubber trees on the vast 100-acre section of jungle, making small incisions in the bark. He would then place a leaf directly under the incision to catch the latex that would drop out of the trees bark in throughout the mid-morning. By noon he went back to each tree, carefully taking the contents of each leaf and pouring the tiny droplets into a bucket. By the afternoon, he would process the rubber into flat sheets, bundle them together, and set them out for the owner to pick up.

This was Andrés' work day after day after day. It was hard, slow, and monotonous work. Such work all but forces one to drift deep into personal contemplation. The young man intensely contemplated the questions that haunt the heart of every person.

FORGOTTEN

He later wrote: "It was at a time when I was looking for answers, for meaning in life. I wanted to know where we came from, why we were alive, and where we go after we die. I have lived for almost 20 years, learning the old stories and legends from my father and grandfather. I had looked inside and outside my culture and had found no answers to my longing for truth."

To break the repetition of his work and thoughts, he took out the transistor radio for which he was working so far from home and began to carefully turn its dial, listening for the reception of the invisible signals that floated through the jungle air from places he had never seen. All of a sudden, a strong, clear signal came over the speaker. It was of a man speaking words that he understood. But the almost cryptic message was confusing and startling. The man on the radio quoted the book of God saying, "…the sun (shall) be darkened, and the moon shall not give her light, and the stars shall fall from heaven, and the powers of the heavens shall be shaken: And then shall appear the sign of the Son of man in heaven: and then shall all the tribes of the earth mourn, and they shall see the Son of man coming in the clouds of heaven with power and great glory."

The menacing handful of sentences overshadowed whatever was to follow by the voice on the radio. For the next several hours, Andrés wondered what was being described. What was this God saying? Can He really do what He said? Darken the sun and darken the moon? Cause the stars to fall from the heavens? None of the gods of his father had ever suggested such power.

As he thought about these things evening turned into night, and that is when it happened. Just as the book of God had said from the man on the radio, the moon did not give its light! He found

ANDRES OF THE MUINANE TRIBE

himself in a jungle of complete darkness. You see, that very night in complete happenstance, the thick forests of South America were thrown into darkness by a lunar eclipse. The event was forever imprinted on the mind of Andrés. With great fear and awe, he was convinced that the message was real from the voice on the radio. He said, "I did not understand much of what the man said, but I knew that the book he read contained truth. I had to find that book! I had to find the truth."

Not long after, Andrés came back at his home near the Caquetá River. As soon as he arrived, he received a message that his grandfather back home in the village of La Sabana was dying. Immediately Andrés set out on the three days walk to his hometown, hoping it was not too late to see his grandfather one last time.

Six months earlier, despite the shock and confusion of all their family and friends, Jim and Jan Walton, along with two-year-old son Danny and three-year-old daughter Diana, left the cold of Minnesota and the comfort of America, to follow the call of God into the jungles of Columbia. They spent the following months trying to adjust to a brand new day-to-day existence; along with an arduous three-month Spanish crash course, and an intense prayer to know where God wanted them to go. Finally, God seemed to direct them to the tribe of the Muinane people in the small village of La Sabana.

On July 3, 1963, Jim Walton and fellow missionary Stan Schauer set out for a Catholic Mission in Loma Linda where Muinane children were brought to learn the Spanish language. After a 175-mile seaplane ride into the jungles of the Amazon rainforest, Jim and Stan arrived at Loma Linda. The Catholic priest and nuns were gracious to their guests; feeding and offering a place to rest for the night. As Jim and Stan discussed with them where they were going in hopes finding a guide to La Sabana, they discovered that the chief of the Muinane people, Chief Fernando, had arrived at the mission just a few days earlier to escort some of the Muinane children back to the village of La Sabana. With a proper introduction and some exchanged pleasantries, the Muinane chief agreed to guide them back to his home.

After a two day arduous hike through the hills of the rainforest, they arrived at La Sabana where the two missionaries collapsed from exhaustion into the hammocks of a guest hut.

The next morning, Jim was awakened by the sound of songbirds. He walked out of the hut with a New Testament in hand to get in some morning devotion. A few children spotted him and asked if he would read the book to them in English. Jim began to read First John chapter four in English. The little children cackled with laughter at the sound of the strange language. Jim tried to explain some of the words to them in Spanish, but could tell right away that he was barely understood. Without a doubt, Jim would have to learn the Muinane language.

Standing nearby was a young man, in his twenties, staring intently at Jim. He was apparently interested in what Jim was reading, but at the same time uncertain, being sure to keep his distance. In Spanish, the young man asked, "What book is that?" Jim replied, "It is the Bible." "What is it about?" the young man asked. "It is God's Word, and this book is one of the reasons I want to come and live here. I want to learn your language and someday translate this book for your people."

ANDRES OF THE MUINANE TRIBE

The young man just continued his gaze at Jim, seemingly wanting to ask more questions, yet holding his peace. Then he abruptly turned and walked away. This young man was Chief Fernando's son, Andrés; who had arrived breathlessly at the village just the day before to be at the bedside of his dying grandfather.

Andrés later said, "When I saw you reading that book, I knew it was the book – the book from the radio, the book that had the truth. And when you said it was God's Word, and you wanted to put it in my language, I determined to help you." It was not long after while trying to help Jim Walton translate that book of truth for the Muinane people; that truth broke into the heart of Andrés who came to personal faith in Jesus Christ. And for the next 18 years, Andrés did assist Jim Walton in translating a first draft of the entire New Testament; a summary of the Old Testament scriptures into the Muinane language; and help introduce the gospel of Jesus Christ to an isolated tribe in the Amazon jungle.

It is also interesting to note that three years earlier, in August of 1961, the Lord spoke to the heart of a man by the name of Dr. Paul Freed. He was then the president of the Trans World Radio. He had a vision of communicating the gospel through the radio to Central and South American countries. This vision led him to Puerto Rico in February of 1962 in hopes of opening a sub-power station to send the message of Jesus Christ to millions of people in the jungles of Central and South America. Construction of the transmitter and station began in September of 1963 on the little Caribbean island of Bonaire and by August of 1964 Spanish speaking Christian programming was in full swing. The radio message that Andrés heard in June or July of 1964 must have been one of the first test broadcasts of this Trans World Radio project from the station at Bonaire.

FORGOTTEN

Can God reach into the darkest jungle with the light of the gospel? Can God carry His message into a place that it has never been? Can God relocate a person to place them in line with a head-on collision with His truth? Can God take to a blinded heart the only name that can bring sight? Can God order the events of time and space, delaying some things, and expediting others to orchestrate the unthinkable? Can God take unrelated lives and tune them together into a harmony of His praise and exaltation? Can God really do all this? Jeremiah 32:27 gives God's response:

Behold, I am the LORD, the God of all flesh: is there any thing too hard for me? (Jeremiah 32:27)

GENESIUS OF ROME

My wife and I were at a retreat; gathered together with a group of cancer survivors playing one of those "get to know each other" games. A pile of index cards lay on the floor, each one having some in-depth question to answer. It was my turn. I picked the card up, and the question was this, "What in your life would you most like to let go of if you could?" I immediately made a joke: "This card!" and dropped it to the floor. Everybody chuckled a little.

But I got a look of anticipation from the facilitator, so my mind began to quickly swirl. I blurted out the first thing that came to mind: "I wish that I could let go of the desire to want to control my kids." I elaborated by telling the group that I see the path that my children are taking. It was the same path that I took, and I know where it ends. I want them to make a detour and bypass all the regrets and mistakes that I made. I want to make them do, what I know is best for them. I wish I could just let go of that. The group got a little silent, in somewhat of an agreement.

FORGOTTEN

After the discussion, my wife and I were talking to the facilitator, and I said, "When God changed my life, it was like a lightning strike. No rhyme or reason to it. It was not predictable. It just happened seemingly out of nowhere. I don't want to depend on lightning strikes to get my children's attention."

I believe this moment in my life captures the frustration that every parent must feel from time to time. Even more so the Christian parent. We want our descendants to know the same God that we do, in the same powerful way that we have come to know him. But we don't want to have to depend on lightning. Lightning is unpredictable, it's unexpected, and it's uncontrollable.

What I had to come to grips with was this truth: Yes, lightning is all that. It is unpredictable, unexpected, and uncontrollable. It is also dangerous, powerful, and instantaneous. But lightning does lay in the hands of God. He directs lightning as it pleases Him. He also breaks into the lives of individuals when and where he will. He proved that in my life, confronting me on a late night drive in the middle of my college years. And he has done it in countless lives since.

In AD303, God confronted a most vile and blasphemous young man who had strayed far from the instruction of family. And He did so, at not a more inconvenient moment.

- ೞ)ಛ -

The persecutions of Christians had reached a fevered pitch during the reign of Roman Emperor Diocletian. Although Christianity had been the focus of oppression in general since its inception, Emperor Diocletian, who was committed to the traditional Roman pantheon of gods, declared state-sanctioned persecution of Christians. On the 23rd of February AD 303, he ordered that the newly built church at Nicomedia be wholly destroyed. He demanded that its scriptures be burned, and all of its assets seized and added to the national treasury.

On the very next day, Diocletian's first "Edict against the Christians" was published. It ordered the destruction of Christian scriptures and all places of worship across the empire and also prohibited Christians from assembling for worship. Christians were hunted like wild animals over all the realm. Once captured and unwilling to renounce their allegiance to Jesus Christ, they would subject to any number of tortures. They would be scourged until the flesh would be ripped from their bones. Then to magnify the pain, the wounds were rubbed with salt and vinegar.

Others were placed on racks and pulled until their bones were ripped out of joint. Some were fed to the lions as entrainment at sporting events. Over 20,000 Christians are estimated to have died during Diocletian's reign of terror.

Emperor Diocletian demanded that every soldier in the entire Roman army perform a sacrifice to the gods or face discharge. One prominent story from the Diocletian persecution was that of a Roman soldier named George, who loudly renounced the Emperor's edict, and in front of his fellow soldiers declared himself to be a Christian by vowing his worship only to Jesus Christ. Diocletian attempted to bribe George to renounce his faith. He offered him lands and wealth if he would but make one sacrifice to the gods of Rome. George adamantly refused and was subjected to the cruelest of torture that ended in his decapitation.

FORGOTTEN

Needless to say, society as a whole viewed Christianity with disdain. As in the early days of Christian persecution by Nero, Christians were blamed for any disasters or destructions that took place. Twice in the reign of Emperor Diocletian, the Imperial Palace was burned. Each time, Christians were accused of a conspiracy to kill the Emperor. Following the lead of the Emperor, culture itself was permeated with an anti-Christian sentiment.

Genesius of Rome was one who looked to profit from this anti-Christian bias. He was a gifted actor, comedian, playwright and the leader of a troupe of actors in Rome. In the summer of AD 303, Emperor Diocletian was set to make a rare visit to Rome to celebrate the 20th anniversary of his reign as Caesar. Numerous civic and cultural events were being organized to commemorate his visit. Knowing of Diocletian's disdain for Christianity, Genesius decided to write a comedy, a play mocking Christianity. There is some speculation that he hoped to gain favor with the Emperor through the excess of his mockery of Christians, and be granted some sort of appointed position in his court.

Although he had some knowledge of the Christian faith because some of his own family, (most likely his mother and father) had been converted to Christ, Genesius had repudiated its teaching long ago. He needed to know more of this hated religion. To research his play, he approached members of the underground church in Rome as if he was a new convert. He was able to convince Christian leaders that he was earnest in his belief and wanted to know more of the Christian faith and be baptized. He went through a period of instruction, keenly interested in the subject of baptism and its picture of the washing away of sins. Roman culture had a love for water and bathing which would be captivating to an audience. Genesius kept up the charade until he was satisfied he had enough information to devise his theatrical production, and then he abandoned his Christian teacher.

He assembled his troop and explained his play to them. It would be centered on the act of baptism. Through the scenes they would make fun of various aspects of the Christian faith, the punchline would be when Genesius would be baptized on stage. The roles of priests, exorcists, and guards were set, and all was ready to make an excellent impression on the Emperor.

The play itself began with Genesius acting in the lead role as a sick man lying on a bed. He is calling his friends to bring him something to relieve his suffering. When they had done all that they could, he said that he felt that he was soon to die, and was resolved to, "die a Christian that God may receive me on this day of my death as One who seeks his salvation by flying from idolatry and superstition." A priest and an exorcist were called asking him what he would have them do. Genesius said to them, "I desire to receive the grace of Jesus Christ and to be born again that I may be delivered from my sins." With the crowd snickering at his lines, something began to change in the heart of this actor with these words.

As the play continued, the priest and the exorcist carried on with their antics leading Genesius to the waters of baptism. The Emperor and all the company were laughing hysterically at the lunacy of the scene. But in the heart of Genesius, a flood of memory began to wash over his mind. Memories of family relatives and his parents' faith began to surface. A belief that he had long since left behind. Recollections of his recent teachers that had in full faith received and taught him in the way of Christ Jesus and his forgiveness of sins.

FORGOTTEN

It was then that he envisioned a company of bright angels over his head who read out of a book every sin that he had committed from his childhood to the present. Then the book was plunged into cleansing waters and made whiter than snow. It was then and there, before the gawking eyes of Roman high society and the Emperor himself, God sent a lightning bolt of mercy and grace into the receptive heart of this play-actor. And right there on stage, as the performance went on all around him, Genesius received Jesus Christ as his Lord and Saviour.

His acting troop had no idea at what had just taken place. They were all going about with their comic exaggerations. After the baptism, two cast-members dressed as Roman soldiers were to take the drenched convert into custody. These soldiers were to present Genesius to the Emperor for the hilarious climax of the play, but what took place next was intensely dramatic.

As he stood face to face with the great persecutor of Christians, Genesius said, "I came here today to please an earthly Emperor, but what I have done is to please a heavenly King. I came here to give you laughter, but what I have done is to give joy to God and His angels. From this moment on, believe me, I will never mock these great mysteries again. Wherefore, I advise you O great and mighty emperor and all ye people here present who have ridiculed these mysteries, to believe with me that Jesus Christ is the true Lord; that he is the light and the truth and that it is through him you may obtain the forgiveness of your sins."

Diocletian was thrown into a fit of rage at the unsuspecting turn of events and ordered not only Genesius but the entire troupe to be arrested. One by one the other actors were released by thoroughly convincing their captors that they had nothing to do with Christianity and had no idea what had come over their colleague. But through the subsequent questioning and threatening, Genesius continued to profess his new found faith in Jesus Christ.

When he was not persuaded to recant, he was handed over to the Prefect of the Praetorium, who tortured him mercilessly so that he would deny Christ and offer sacrifice to the Roman gods. Genesius was beaten with rods, stretched and pulled on the rack, lacerated with iron hooks, and burned with torches. Through it all, Genesius held fast to his testimony of Jesus Christ as Lord.

During his painful suffering, he is reported to have said, "There is no other Lord of the universe besides Him whom I have seen Him I adore and serve and to Him, I will adhere though I should suffer a thousand deaths for His sake. No torments shall remove Jesus Christ from my heart or mouth." After a great length of agonizing suffering, he was finally condemned to death and was beheaded. His last words are believed to have been: "Our Lord Jesus Christ is God, and we shall have life in His name."

What took place on that Roman stage is a testimony to the saving power of God to reach anyone, anywhere, and at any time. Even the most blackened heart of blasphemy is a candidate for God's miraculous deliverance from sin! Even the most cynical of skeptics can, in a moment's notice, be struck with a deep fear of facing God in judgment with all their sins laid bare before Him. No prodigal son has traveled the road of riotous living too far; no wandering daughter's path lay outside the grasp of God. No father is too hardened; no mother too broken for God to intervene.

FORGOTTEN

I have often heard this Bible verse quoted to parents: Proverbs 22:6: "Train up a child in the way he should go: and when he is old, he will not depart from it." Many, I believe, have misunderstood this verse. This is not a promise that every child raised in a godly home, instructed in the ways of God, loved in line with the character of God, will come back to God. No. Many stray from God never to return. But what the verse says is that they will never get away from Him. He will always be with them. God will ever be there; whether like me, speeding down the highway or like Genesius acting in a play, no matter how far one may roam, they will never cease to hear the inviting echo of the voice of God calling them to Himself.

STUART HAMBLEN

Stuart had been up all night. He had tossed and turned unable to sleep. All he could hear in the back of his mind were the words of that country preacher; about standing before God and giving an account for his life. And his life was a mess. His drinking was taking over. If he landed in jail one more time, he could lose everything. If something didn't happen soon, he would lose it all anyway. But all of that didn't matter a hill of beans when it came to dying. All his popularity and fame, all of his money wouldn't change the fact that he was unprepared to meet God. Then there was Jesus dying on the cross, a bloody scene so hard to imagine and yet so passionately declared by the preacher.

"What am I going to do?" he thought. "What about my career, my reputation? Everything could all fall apart and then what would I do? But compared to eternity, these were nothing." It was at that point that the tears began to roll down his cheeks. His sobs awakened his wife, Suzy. "What's the matter, honey?" "I don't know. I don't know." "Honey, you're scaring me. Now tell me what's going on." "Baby, I can't keep going on like this. Call that preacher Billy, he's staying over at the Langham. I've got to talk to him. I've got to settle this tonight."

- ∽⟩⟨∾ -

In 1949, Billy Graham's Los Angeles evangelistic crusade was off to a sluggish start. Even though he had held a press conference to announce the series of meetings, very few if any of the local papers were talking about the event. Hoping to help the meeting, Presbyterian Bible teacher Henrietta Mears, a supporter of Graham, invited him to her Beverly Hills home to speak to a group of Hollywood personalities of the day.

One of those present was the rowdy ruckus star of cowboy westerns, Stuart Hamblen. Hamblen had played lead roles in some of the many cowboy westerns of the early days of Hollywood. He shared the spotlight as a singing cowboy with famous actors such as Gene Autry, Roy Rogers, and John Wayne. But Hamblen's life off screen had become a reflection of the hard-living cowboy that he portrayed on screen. He was known for his excessive drinking, gambling, and fighting, ending up in the county lock-up on several occasions. Hamblen jokingly referred to himself as the "original juvenile delinquent." But what was happening to his career was no joke. By 1949, Hamblen's wild lifestyle was severely affecting his life and career.

That was what made the encounter with Billy Graham so unusual. The preacher and the Prodigal (Hamblen was the son of a Methodist Minister) hit it off at this chance encounter and became

STUART HAMBLEN

fast friends. Not only was Stuart an actor, but he also hosted one of the most listened-to afternoon radio programs in Los Angeles, and as a result of their meeting, he invited Billy to come on the radio with him and promote the crusade. He agreed knowing that this was a huge break for the crusade.

After their introduction at Henrietta Mears home, Billy developed a burden for Stuart and was praying that he would come to faith in Christ. While on the radio, Stuart warmly conversed with the budding evangelist and encouraged his listeners to come on out to the crusade. During the interview, Graham personally invited Stuart to come to the meeting as well and Stuart said he would.

He was true to his word. Stuart and his wife Suzy came several times during the three-week crusade. But by the end of the three weeks, despite Billy's prayers and earnest preaching, Stuart made no indication that he even remotely considered coming to faith in Christ.

As the scheduled three weeks was coming to a close, the local crusade organizers felt that it had not reached its intended impact. Only in the last few days was it showing signs of momentum. They approached Billy about extending the meeting a few more days.

Although Billy had been in evangelism a couple of years, he had never been approached about extending a meeting. Retreating into a time of prayer with God, he felt as though he needed some kind of indication from the Lord as to what to do. Like Gideon of the Old Testament and his fleece, he asked God for a sign, something that would leave little doubt as to what the Lord wanted him to do.

FORGOTTEN

One night, just before the end of the crusade, Billy was awakened by a phone call at 4:30 in the morning. It was Stuart Hamblen, and he was an emotional wreck, crying uncontrollably. He begged to see Billy as soon as possible, and without hesitation, Billy invited him over.

As Hamblen made his way over to the Langham Hotel, Billy along with his wife Ruth, awakened the evangelistic team and asked them to gather together in prayer for Stuart to be saved. It wasn't long before Stuart and Suzy arrived to meet with Graham, and by mornings light, Stuart put his faith and trust in Christ.

That day marked a transformation in the life of Stuart Hamblen. He spoke of his conversion to Christ on the radio. All of Los Angeles heard of what God had done for the rugged cowboy the night before. Local papers picked up the story, and it wasn't long before all the town was talking about what had happened to the radio cowboy.

The news of Hamblen's conversion marked a turning point in the Los Angeles crusade. From this moment on, crowds swelled night after night. More and more were coming to Christ. Billy Graham took the conversion of Hamblen as the sign from God for which he was asking. The meeting was extended for another five weeks.

By the end of the crusade, through the incessant coverage in newspapers and magazines, Billy Graham became a household name. Later Graham called Hamblen's conversion "the turning point" in the Billy Graham Evangelistic Association's ministry, launching them onto a world-wide stage.

STUART HAMBLEN

Not long after the crusade was over, Stuart ran into an old friend on the streets of Los Angeles. His friend, another cowboy movie star, John Wayne, had caught wind of all the commotion and how the man had changed his ways. Wayne asked, "What's this I hear about you, Stuart?" Stuart replied, "Well, Duke, it's no secret what God can do. What he has done for me, He can do for my friends too." Wayne smiled and said, "That sounds an awful lot like a song."

And sure enough, later that day at his piano, Stuart Hamblen sat down and wrote:

> *It is no secret, what God can do.*
> *What he's done for others, He'll do for you.*
> *With arms wide open, He'll pardon you.*
> *It is no secret what God can do.*

CHARLOTTE ELLIOTT

In his book, The Problem with Pain the Christian author and apologist C.S. Lewis said, "Pain insists upon being attended to. God whispers to us in our pleasures, speaks in our conscience, but shouts in our pain: it is His megaphone to rouse a deaf world." Even the most hardened in unbelief are tempted to lash out at the steely blue heavens and cry "Why God?" when the body is racked with pain or disease.

According to the Bible, the Devil himself knows this. In the ancient and somewhat enigmatic book of Job, after he took all that Job possessed, his wealth by destruction and theft and his children by death, Satan confidently told God "...touch his bone and his flesh, and he will curse thee to thy face." He was wrong of course, but the questions of Job's suffering sparked the tangle of the 40 long chapters that followed.

Sickness and suffering, pain and plague seem to be the question to which many default. They ask, "If there is a God, then why is there so much suffering in the world?" This is not a question that is quickly and glibly answered by quoting chapter and verse. Most often such answers ring hollow to the human heart. Philosophical and even theological postulating make a poor balm for soothing the anguished body.

The harsh reality is that the "Why?" of suffering may never be fully and completely known. But we can be assured that our wounds are not wasted; that our suffering is never senseless. And as in the case of Charlotte Elliott, we can take all the questions and the resentments that our pain may distill from deep within the heart and bring them to God. Despite my inner conflict and doubt, I can come to Jesus, just as I am.

- ℰℭ -

While at the dinner table, she sat as straight and proper as a 19th-century aristocrat's daughter was supposed to. She ate her dinner serenely, seeming at peace with the family and guests around the table. But within the confines of her body and mind, there was another story. The searing pain that washed over her torso made lifting the fork of food to her mouth nearly unbearable. The polite dinner chatter with the family's honored guest was beyond irritating while she swallowed the anguish that begged to be released in cries of pain.

She hadn't always been this way. Born March 18, 1789, Charlotte grew up as the privileged daughter of a silk merchant. She was talented and witty. As a young woman, she made a name for herself as a portrait artist and was published to some acclaim as a writer of humorous poetry.

CHARLOTTE ELLIOTT

But somewhere during these early years, sickness began to grip her body. By the time she was 30 years old, the illness had rendered her a bedridden invalid. She described her health battle as an hourly fight against "bodily feelings of almost overpowering weakness and exhaustion..." She admitted to times of debilitating slothfulness, depression, and instability.

Although Charlotte was raised in a Christian home (her grandfather, Rev. Henry Venn, being a somewhat famous evangelical preacher), she began to be hardened to the things of God. She was heard to mutter, "If God loved me, He would not have treated me this way."

Her family, concerned about her embittered condition, invited Dr. Caesar Malan, a young minister and hymn writer from Switzerland to join them for dinner on May of 1822 and try to speak a word to her concerning the state of her soul.

As the dinner went on, with the family and minister at the table, Charlotte could barely stand another moment. Then, in a lull of the conversation which had turned to spiritual matters, Dr. Malan turned to the austere Charlotte and asked if she knew herself to be truly a Christian, possessing the peace of God. With the question, she knew that the evening was nothing but a ploy, devised by her continually badgering parents, to elicit some sort of spiritual response from her.

In a loud and sharp tone that sent the room into silence, she told the good minister that she resented the question considering it rude and unkind; and that the subject of religion was a matter that she did not wish to discuss at all this evening. The furious outburst was more than her family could bear. Charlotte's heartbroken and embarrassed mother and father soon left the table, followed by her siblings; leaving the red-faced Charlotte alone with the minister to finish the meal. Dr. Malan, in a tone of Christ-like kindness, replied that he would not pursue a subject which so displeased her, but would pray that she might give her heart to Christ, and employ her exceptional talents, with which He had gifted her, to his holy and spiritual use.

The evening may have passed, but the few words that Dr. Malan spoke to her did not. In the days following the dinner that night, Charlotte Elliot found herself in grave concern for her soul and in guilt for her intemperate outburst. Growing up in a Christian home, she knew the claims of Jesus to be the resurrected Son of God. But Charlotte also knew the doubts within her own heart as to why a loving God would allow her to endure such sickness and pain. Secretly, she blamed God for her illness. However, it was He, Jesus, who was said to be the only way to rid herself of sin's guilt and have peace with God. In her tortured state of mind, she turned to the minister, at which, she had so angrily lashed out. She called for Dr. Malan.

Upon his arrival, she apologized for her behavior at dinner a few weeks past and began to pour her heart out to the young pastor. All the resentment and bitterness that she felt within, all the restlessness of mind his words had caused her since their last meeting. Charlotte said, "You speak of coming to Jesus; I want to be saved. I want to come to Jesus, but I don't know how. I'm not fit to come." Dr. Malan answered "Why not come just as you are? Give yourself to God just as you are now, with your fighting's and fears, hates and loves, pride and shame. You have only to come to Him just as you are." And there, amid her crisis of belief, she did come to Jesus, just as she was.

CHARLOTTE ELLIOTT

This moment marked a change in the life of Charlotte Elliott. Although she would be an invalid for the rest of her life and would continue to experience pain and fatigue, the peace and joy in believing on Jesus would be her daily refuge and a constant strength for the rest of her days.

In 1834, Charlotte's brother, Henry Venn Elliott, who by that time had become a minister himself, had a burden to create a school for daughters of clergymen to receive a quality education at a nominal cost. To aid the establishment of what was to be called St. Mary's Hall at Brighton, a bazaar was held, and all of the Elliott household would help.

The day before the bazaar, the whole house was abuzz with activity; everyone preparing decorations and cooking meals; running about with no time to spare, that is except for Charlotte. Unable to move from the chair she had to be helped into, all she could do was watch as others did so much. Once again, Charlotte struggled with the feelings of complete and utter uselessness.

That night, she was kept awake by distressing thoughts of her seeming inability to be used by God to do anything. These thoughts led to further questions of her own faith. Was her faith in vain? Was the trust she had placed on Jesus so long ago, combined with all the feelings of peace, love, and security all for nothing, merely to be dissolved over time?

The next day, the busy day of the bazaar, Charlotte lay upon her sofa still contemplating the vexing questions of the night before. But the new day brought a new resolve. She felt as though these distressing thoughts must be met and conquered by God's grace. Charlotte then began to reflect on the great certainties of her faith

FORGOTTEN

and not of her emotions. In her mind, she went back to that day in 1822 when she conversed with Dr. Malan; the gentleness of Jesus' promise to receive her if she would only come to Him; the peace and pardon that she found in Jesus. Taking pen and paper from a nearby table, Charlotte put into verse, as she was prone to do, somewhat of a formula of her faith as a comfort to her own heart. Her memorable words were:

> *Just as I am - without one plea,*
> *But that Thy blood was shed for me,*
> *And that Thou bidst me come to Thee,*
> *-O Lamb of God, I come!*
>
> *Just as I am - and waiting not*
> *To rid my soul of one dark blot,*
> *To Thee, whose blood can cleanse each spot,*
> *-O Lamb of God, I come!*
>
> *Just as I am - though toss'd about*
> *With many a conflict, many a doubt,*
> *Fightings and fears within, without,*
> *-O Lamb of God, I come!*
>
> *Just as I am - Thou wilt receive,*
> *Wilt welcome, pardon, cleanse, relieve;*
> *Because Thy promise I believe,*
> *-O Lamb of God, I come!*

CHARLOTTE ELLIOTT

Later on that day, her sister-in-law, Mrs. H.V. Elliott, came in to check on her and tell her how the bazaar was going. She saw the slip of paper with her poetic words and immediately realized the beauty of its simple but powerful message and asked if she might make a copy of it. Soon the poem was shared with her brother then printed under the title of "Just as I Am" and sold for the benefit of St. Mary's Hall, Brighton. Thousands were sold, and as a result, the school for girls was fully funded. The invalid who despaired that she could be of no use or help to her brother's endeavor for the Kingdom of God became its greatest benefactor.

Her poem was later set to music by William B. Bradbury, best known for composing the music to the hymn "Jesus Loves Me," and published in numerous hymn books throughout the 19th century. Even today, rare is the Christian hymn book that does not contain this beloved and familiar song.

Now, one cannot overstate the powerful ways in which God has used the hymn Just As I Am. Charlotte Elliott's brother, the Rev. H.V. Elliott said, "In the course of a long ministry I hope I have been permitted to see some fruit for my labors, but I feel far more has been done by a single hymn of my sister's." On his often visits to her sick bed, he was heard to say "You have done more by that one hymn of yours, than I by all my years of preaching."

Of the song, the great evangelist D.L. Moody shared the sentiment of no doubt thousands through history, "It has done the most good to the greatest number, and has touched more lives helpfully than any other hymn." The ministry of world-famous Evangelist Billy Graham has been tied to Elliott's hymn. It has been said that "Just as I Am" was the invitation hymn at Mordecai Hamm's revival meeting in Charlotte, North Carolina when Billy Graham was converted to Christ. Through the decades of his evangelistic crusades, this hymn was the mainstay of his gospel call. Graham said the song presented "the strongest possible Biblical basis for the call of Christ." He even entitled his 1997 autobiography Just As I Am.

Hymnody historian Kenneth Osbeck wrote that "Just as I Am" had "touched more hearts and influenced more people for Christ than any other song ever written." Christian writer Lorella Rouster wrote, "The hymn is an amazing legacy for an invalid woman who suffered from depression and felt useless to God's service." Dr. John Julian wrote, "Though weak and feeble in body, she possessed a strong imagination and a well-cultured and intellectual mind…" Her verse is characterized by the tenderness of feeling, plaintive simplicity, deep devotion, and perfect rhythm. She sang for those in sickness and sorrow as very few others have ever done."

The song even had a powerful effect on the author herself. Several years after the poem was published, Miss Elliott was once again in the office of yet another doctor. She was very sick and once again battling the depression into which her constant pain drove her. The doctor, realizing the low state of her spirit reached over onto his desk and handed her one of the leaflets that had been donated to the doctor's office for just such an occasion. It is said that Charlotte burst into tears of grateful joy when she read the words on the page, for they were her own. Someone who much admired the words had them published and widely distributed them. Charlotte Elliott saw the evidence of how God had used her efforts, despite her feeble frame.

CHARLOTTE ELLIOTT

Not long after her conversion, she stumbled across a verse of scripture in the gospel of John that seemed to the very essence of what Dr. Caesar Malan encouraged her to do that memorable night so long ago. Regardless of all the unanswered questions of her pain and weakness, of her sickness and trouble of mind; regardless of all the doubts, the why's and the how's of her fragile state, regardless of all the anger, resentment and bitter turmoil that raged within her; she could come to Jesus.

This verse containing the words of Jesus that she found so precious then, still rings true for us today. It calls us to come and believe, to lay at the feet of Jesus, all that seems to stand between God and us. It is a verse that beckons us to come near to Him, to unburden our heavy hearts on His strong shoulders; to lay bare our sin before Him, trusting that he will forgive and cleanse it. In the gospel of John Chapter 6 and verse 37, Charlotte Elliott found refuge in Jesus' words:

All that the Father giveth me shall come to me; and him that cometh to me I will in no wise cast out. (John 6:37)

THE BIBLE ON THE BOUNTY

Jack desperately rummaged through all that was taken off of the ship. It seemed like he had done this a thousand times; and each time he did, in his mind he could see the flames of the ship rising higher and higher. It seemed like such a good idea at the time. He, along with all the others, thought that they have found paradise. There were plenty of birds and fruit trees. Shelter could be easily produced. The climate was mild, the ocean breeze was constant, and the uninhabited island held no threat to their life of ease. Everything was perfect.

That was until they started fighting with each other. Squabbles over the native women they had kidnapped were harmless at first. But when one of the crew found a way to distill alcohol from one of the native plants, things only grew worse. On top of this, the slaves they had brought along were becoming more and more difficult to handle. The paradise on which they all thought they wanted to spend the rest of their lives was becoming a nightmare. Something had to change!

That's when Jack opened one of the neglected boxes that had been taken from the HMS Bounty and found a book. Although he couldn't read, he could recognize from its thin pages and columned text, that this was a copy of the Holy Bible. Jack's first thought was about all he had done: the mutiny, the kidnapping, the drunkenness, the illicit sex; the murder. The last thing that he wanted to hear was what that book had to say about his past. But another thought crossed his mind, what if, just what if, there was an answer for his life in that book? What if there was something in that book that could change the perilous direction their tropical community was going? When Jack walked out of the hut with the Bible under his arm, and desperation of mind to try anything, he had no idea that everything was about to change.

- ഗ‍‌ର -

On the 23rd of December 1787, His Majesty's Ship the Bounty sailed from Spithead, England for the South Pacific island of Tahiti, captained by Lieutenant William Bligh of the Royal Navy. Captain Bligh was on a botanical mission for a very unique purpose. He and his crew were sent to the Island of Tahiti to collect saplings of a breadfruit tree; a tree which produced a versatile year-round fruit. The plan was to transport these saplings to the West Indies Islands where the fruit would be a source of cheap food for the slave population on the sugarcane plantations.

THE BIBLE ON THE BOUNTY

The voyage intended to cross the Atlantic, down to the tip of South America and cross into the Pacific at Cape Horn. But upon arriving and waiting for over a month for adverse weather conditions to change, Captain Bligh rerouted the vessel east, approaching the Tahitian Islands by way of the tip of Africa and the Indian Ocean. This change in course greatly exaggerated the length of the voyage. Often tensions were high among the crew. During the journey, Bligh demoted Sailing Master John Fryer, replacing him with Fletcher Christian a non-commissioned officer but a friend of the captain. This act severely damaged relations between the Captain and the already exhausted crew.

By October 1788, the Bounty reached Tahiti. The arrival to this island was the most significant incentive for sailors to sign on for such an extended voyage. Although it was hard, and monotonous on the close confines of the Bounty, it was worth it to spend several months in the arms of a tropical paradise. The climate was glorious, there was plenty to drink, and the native women were, well, extremely friendly.

Bligh allowed the crew to live ashore, collecting and caring for the potted breadfruit plants set to be transported off the island. As they did, the sailors became infused into much of the culture, learning its customs and living among them. The Acting Lieutenant Fletcher Christian even married a Tahitian woman by the name of Maimiti. Several other of the crew became attached to the exotic native beauties.

Needless to say, after they had spent five months on this Polynesian paradise, these sailors were not willing to leave. Several weeks before their departure, three men actually deserted,

FORGOTTEN

stealing some provisions and trying to make a get-away in a smaller rescue boat. They were recovered after a few weeks, and to make an example out of them, Captain Bligh had them flogged. Although there had been more talk of desertion, it was silenced with this show of power. And on April 4th, 1789 the crew grudgingly boarded the Bounty and set sail to deliver their cargo.

But three weeks into the return voyage, things began to be unbearable. Captain Bligh's demeanor had changed. Maybe he could see the effect of such a protracted stay on the crew. They were not the sea-hardened sailors they were before. They were listless and pining away after their previous port. Several incidents put the Captain at odds with Fletcher Christian, upon which he unleashed his unbridled rage on him. Finally, Christian had had enough, feeling his treatment was intolerable. Others of the crew, in a mood of discontent and resentment, saw Fletcher Christian as an ally for drastic action.

In the early morning hours of April 28, with conspirators that he knew would help him, Fletcher Christian instigated a mutiny. Quickly taking control of the storage of arms, he distributed weapons to all of his followers, then arrested the captain. For several minutes, the Bounty was in chaos with the sound of screams and shouts, of cursing and jeering. There were scenes of fighting and threats, struggles and tussles among the crew.

Finally, things calmed down as the mutineers, although outnumbered, had taken the boat. Christian's men prepared the ship's largest rescue boat for Bligh and those loyal to the captain, supplying it with five days' worth of food and water, a sextant, compass, and nautical tables, as well as a tool chest. By 10 o'clock in the morning, the captain and his men were loaded onto the boat and set out to fend for themselves in the middle of the Pacific Ocean. Miraculously though, Bligh led the men on an arduous 3,500-mile journey to the Dutch settlement of Kupang. They arrived 47 days later, having only lost one man in death.

The Bounty, however, now under the command of Fletcher Christian, returned to the island of Tahiti where the crew resumed their care-free lifestyle. But after a while, there became a haunting concern about being discovered by English authorities. No one knew what had happened to the hard-nosed Captain Bligh. Could he have possibly survived? Could he, at that very moment, be assembling a crew of the Royal Navy to come after the mutineers and bring them to justice? A mutiny was a capital offense. They were all subject to being hanged.

Although 16 of the mutineers stayed behind in Tahiti taking their chances that the authorities wouldn't find them, Christian along with 8 other crewmen, decided to once again board the Bounty and to sail east in search of an uncharted island where they could live out their days without the fear of Bligh's revenge. Before leaving, they lured 6 Tahitian men, and 11 women with one baby out onto the bounty, kidnapping them onto their voyage.

Fletcher Christian and the crew made their way through the Fiji and Cook Islands, realizing that they would indeed be secondary targets for the Royal Navy's search. They continued until they reached on Pitcairn Island on January 15, 1790. According to the maps in their possession, the island had been misplaced. Its location was a full 216 miles east of where it was marked out on the map making it nearly impossible to intentionally find.

FORGOTTEN

The island was uninhabited. Its craggy shores and pristine wilderness beckoned them to forge a new life safely hidden from their past. Upon exploring the Island, it was found to be in abundance of coconuts, breadfruit trees, and other useful crops along with plenty of fresh water and fertile land. Having decided that this would be their new home, they unloaded everything from the Bounty, stripped it of anything that might prove useful, and burned the ship in the bay. They did this so that no passing ship would be drawn to the vessel in the harbor and to prevent anyone from leaving the island and perchance reveal their location. On January 23, 1790, they watched as the Bounty, engulfed in flames, sank into the sea.

This was the life they longed for; the life they dreamed of; the life they committed treason for on the high seas: A tropical paradise, exotic women, plenty of food and water and enough slaves to do the work for them. But these elements, coupled with the discovery of an alcoholic brew made from the root of one of the island plants, created a toxic combination.

Things were peaceable at first, and everyone seemed to slip into a co-existent life, but over time the six Tahitian men began to deeply resent their treatment as slaves and the abuse of the eleven women who were being passed around among the crew as sexual concubines. Then there were jealousies and bad blood among the sailors over the possession of the women. Fletcher Christian's leadership had diminished in authority over the years.

Anger erupted into violence in September 1793, when the remaining Tahitian slaves conducted a series of attacks on the crew members. In that month 5 of the crew members from the

THE BIBLE ON THE BOUNTY

Bounty were killed, including Fletcher Christian who was working in the fields when he was shot and then butchered with an ax.

For the next several months, an uneasy tension pervaded the island. In fighting broke out between the 6 Tahitian men and by 1794 all of them were dead either by the hand of each other or by the widows of the dead mutineers. This left four remaining from the crew of the Bounty: Ned Young, Alexander Smith (who changed his name to Jack Adams to obscure his identity), William McCoy, and Matthew Quintal.

Young and Adams began to assert control over the inhabitants of the island. But often that control was disordered by the wild drunken behavior of McCoy and Quintal. For several years they lived in an uneasy fear that what took place before would happen again. In 1798, McCoy, in a drunken frenzy, killed himself by jumping off a cliff with a stone tied around his neck. Quintal, slipping further and further into a life of a perpetual alcoholic stupor, threatened to massacre the whole community.

This threat proved to be too much for Young and Adams to just overlook as idle talk. By then, they had deep roots in this community, each with several children. So not long after the threat was made, Young and Adams both attacked Quintal with an ax and murdered him.

It was supposed to be a dream-like tropical paradise, but it had turned into a nightmare of debauchery and murder. By this time, there were two remaining mutineers, 9 women, and 19 children. This weighed heavy on the mind of Jack Adams: What would become of this community? Will these children grow up only to abuse and kill each other? Something had to change.

It was this uncertainty about the future that sent him to the small hut that contained the remains of all that was taken from the Bounty before she was sunk. It was there that Adams found a locker containing a Bible which had been presented to the HMS Bounty by the Naval and Military Bible Society before setting sail from England so long ago. He also found a copy of the Book of Common Prayer, a useful guide to worship in the Church of England.

Adams was an uneducated man who could not read, but Ned Young, who was an officer cadet on the Bounty, did know how to read. Jack took the books to Ned, who began to, not only recite them aloud but teach Adams to read for himself. It was urgent that he do this right away because, in 1799, Ned Young was showing signs of tuberculosis, also called consumption. His health quickly deteriorated, and by the end of 1800, he died.

But not before he, along with Adams, were wholly transformed in mind and heart by what they read in that surviving Bible from the Bounty. Although he stood as the lone man on the island after the death of Young, Jack Adams knew that the truth presented in this book could bring peace and stability to their once volatile community.

Adams poured over the Bible, reading it again and again, drinking in its wisdom and drawing nearer to God in worship. He set out to instill the truths of God's word in the minds of the many children of the island by starting a school to teach the children how to read using the Bible as their textbook. Jack instituted Sunday worship where he preached the scriptures, taught them spiritual disciplines, and personal devotion to God. He insisted that thanks be given to God before and after every meal and set up daily times of corporate prayer.

One of the prayers he had written in a journal is a testimony to his deep heartfelt love for God: "Suffer me not, O Lord, to waste this day in sin or folly. But Let me worship thee with much delight. Teach me to know more of thee and to serve thee better than ever I have done before, that I may be fitter to dwell in heaven, where thy worship and service are everlasting. Amen."

Over the years to come, this now firmly Christian community left behind the distant memories of bloody conflict and hedonistic living. It became a tranquil village centered on devotion to Jesus Christ and genuine love for one another. In February 1808, by happenstance, an American seal hunting vessel named the Topaz spotted what seemed to be an uncharted island. When they landed, they were met with natives that surprisingly spoke a muddled English dialect.

Captain of the Topaz, Mayhew Folger, soon met the only white man on the island, Jack Adams, who confessed that he was the last of the mutineers from the HMS Bounty. This was shocking enough, but even more so was what had developed on the island over the years. The island was inhabited by thirty-five literate English-speaking people of Polynesian descent who were practicing the Christian faith. They lived a life of piety, praying together morning and evening. Uncharacteristically of native tribes, they lived in peace, expressing goodwill and kindness toward one another. And the sexual promiscuity so prevalent in their culture was absent.

They regularly worshipped together and could recite the Apostles' Creed and sections of scripture from memory. One observer wrote, "In conducting the most trivial affairs, they are guided by the Scriptures, which they have read diligently, and from which they quote with freedom and frequency..." Another early witness wrote: "It was with great gratification that we observed the Christian simplicity of the natives. They appeared to have no guile. Their cottages were open to all, and all were welcome to their food."

Eventually, word of the discovery, of the last mutineer from the HMS Bounty made its way to England where British warships were sent to arrest Adams, but upon arriving and finding its astounding community whose welfare was wholly dependent upon the aged mutineer, they refused to remove him from Pitcairn Island. When they reported their findings back to England, the Royal Navy Command decided to take no action. Jack Adams died on March 5th, 1829, surrounded by a grateful community.

In its fundamental essence, the Bible is a collection of 66 books written by about 40 authors, in three different languages, over a time period of approximately 1600 years. It is also the most reproduced book of all time. And although many have done their best down through the centuries to drive its pages from existence, it persists unto this very day. The indestructibility of the Bible is due in large part to its power to change the hearts and minds of people. The Bibles words of truth untangle the thoughts of the deceived. Its divine lines illuminate the darkened path of life to genuine communion with God.

What took place on an island lost in the middle of the Pacific Ocean in a moment of complete desperation is a testimony to the power of the word of God. In the ancient prophecy of Isaiah God has given great assurance as to the ability of His word saying:

For as the rain cometh down, and the snow from heaven, and returneth not thither, but watereth the earth, and maketh it bring forth and bud, that it may give seed to the sower, and bread to the eater: So shall my word be that goeth forth out of my mouth: it shall not return unto me void, but it shall accomplish that which I please, and it shall prosper in the thing whereto I sent it. (Isaiah 55:10-11)

THE KING OF CHATTANOOGA

1932. Times probably couldn't have gotten any worse. The impact of Black Tuesday, the Wall Street crash of '29, had made its way all across the country. Jobs were scarce. Unemployment rose to 33%. Factories were closing everywhere. Money was tight. In the breadbasket of the nation, a dust bowl was brewing. The heavens were shut up, and the farmlands were wasting away. Desperation and fear spread like a disease.

Prohibition was over a decade old now. And the gleaming promises of Evangelist Billy Sunday, the voice of the temperance movement crying in the wilderness, that through Prohibition, "The slums will soon be only a memory. We will turn our prisons into factories and our jails into storehouses and corncribs..." never really came to pass. It became the classic case of unintended consequences. The insatiable thirst for booze never really went away, it just went underground. The tentacles of organized crime, which had always been there, just below the surface of social respectability, reached farther and deeper than ever before. The black market for alcohol flourished and along with prostitution, gambling, and theft. With this came the rise in violence, burglaries, homicides, and assaults that had law enforcement at their wit's end. Newspapers were filled with stories of the dodgy exploits of crime bosses in the cities of New York and Chicago. Around this time Al Capone, not Mayor Anton Cermak, was the King of Chicago and he ruled the town with an iron fist.

Men like Capone, crime bosses that had a stranglehold of power through criminal activity, were in cities all over America. Chattanooga, Tennessee was no exception. It had its own crime boss that kept his finger on the pulse of a dark underworld in this sleepy southern town. Chattanooga had its king of crime. That is, until one summer night when the King of Chattanooga was overthrown by the King of kings.

- ಬಇ -

Mordecai Ham was an American Independent Baptist evangelist of the early 20th Century. He was born April 2, 1877, and entered the ministry in 1901. There were more than 33,000 conversions during the first year of his work in evangelism, and more than 300,000 new converts joined Baptist churches in Georgia, Alabama, Mississippi, Tennessee, Kentucky, and the Carolinas in the space of 30 years. He held evangelistic crusades all over the United States for decades.

He was a man that often found himself at odds with townspeople, especially those who did not support the temperance movement. Ham was a strong supporter of prohibition. In 1908 Ham was preaching in Salisbury, North Carolina, where a State Prohibition election was to be held. The night before the election Ham had to be escorted to and from the tabernacle by armed guards. After the service, the men paraded through the streets all night shouting, "Hang Ham! Hang Ham!" As he left by train, a U.S. Marshall had to stand outside on the station platform holding two pistols pointed at the crowd.

His life was threatened numerous times. He was assaulted by what seemed like random attackers and maligned by city administrations. Once in 1927, as he was crossing the street, he was struck down by an automobile and dragged for half a block. It was never really determined whether it was an accident or a deliberate attempt on his life.

But with all the risks and dangers of his bold gospel preaching came a harvest of souls. Close observers wrote concerning Mordecai Ham, "He exalts Christ and fights sin with all his might. There is no middle ground in his campaigns. Evaluating the impact of his ministry is impossible. Under his preaching I have seen murderers saved, drunkards converted, homes reunited, and men and women dedicate their lives to special service." His biography is a long list of remarkable individual stories of conversions.

Mordecai Ham would often follow a similar pattern when beginning a city campaign. When he came into a city, he would focus on the most notorious sinner in town, and win that one to Jesus Christ; and then most of the community would follow suit. Once he confronted an infidel, who was hiding in a cornfield to avoid the preacher. "What are you going to do?" asked this opponent of the gospel. "Ask God to kill you," replied Ham. The infidel protested. Ham said that since the man claimed to believe there was no God, such a prayer shouldn't bother him in the least. Nonetheless, the unbeliever begged Ham not to pray for his death, and so Ham agreed to pray for his salvation instead, and the man was converted on the spot.

In January of 1933, Ham opened a campaign in Little Rock, Arkansas, and set his sights on a man by the name of Otto Sutton. He was a wild, worldly, wicked and reckless heavyweight fighter at the time. And not long after the meeting began, he was converted to Christ. He later became the pastor of the Valence Street Baptist Church of New Orleans, Louisiana.

One of the most notable converts of Mordecai Ham was a tall North Carolina teenager in 1934. Ham was preaching a revival on the outskirts of Charlotte, where some 6400 people were converted to Christ during the crusade. One of those was a young Billy Graham. The teenager was amazed as he saw more than 5,000 in every meeting, and every seat was filled. People were getting saved all around him. It seemed to the young man that the only place safe from the evangelist's wrath was the choir and that's where he and his friend, Grady Wilson, sat the next night. The evangelist's first words were, "There's a great sinner in this place tonight." Billy thought to himself, "Mother's been telling him about me." Later that evening, during the close of the service, he turned to Grady and said, "Let's go!" Billy Graham put his trust in the Lord Jesus that night.

In 1932, Mordecai Ham had started a revival in Chattanooga Tennessee. One night of the meeting, to keep a promise he had made to his little girl, a man by the name of Wyatt Larimore went to the Chattanooga meeting.

Larimore was known as the "King" of the Chattanooga underworld. He was a racketeer and thick in the bootlegging business. According to his own testimony, Larimore had stood before the courts of Hamilton County for every conceivable crime, ranging from traffic violations to first-degree murder. At the time, he was paying taxes on more than $200,000, much of which was obtained from his illicit businesses; chains of bootleg distilleries and gambling houses, which were managed by more than 300 men who worked under him.

On the night that Wyatt Larimore was in the meeting, Mordecai Ham preached on "God's Last Call." Larimore came under great conviction, and after several days of mental and spiritual despair, He went back to the meeting and was thoroughly converted. On the night that Larimore was saved, many of the 300 men that worked under him were saved as well. In the following days, Larimore went back to the whole crew and said, "Boy's we are through. We're going to close all the rackets and bust all this rotten liquor." For some time after his conversion, he made his living peddling fish on the streets of Chattanooga. But, the Lord used him in the lives of many, many people and it is said that he gave his testimony in every Church in Chattanooga."

The astonishing story of Wyatt Larimore's transformation is a testimony to the life-changing power of Jesus Christ. The blackest and darkest of sin can be forgiven by the redemptive work of God's Son on the cross of Calvary. If the kings of sin and rebellion will yield their thrones to the Prince of Glory, real genuine change

FORGOTTEN

can take place in the heart and mind. A transformation as different as night and day. And as the Old Testament prophet Isaiah said:

…Though your sins be as scarlet, they shall be as white as snow; though they be red like crimson, they shall be as wool. (Isaiah 1:18)

MARTYRS

WILLIAM HUNTER

We all feel something special when someone close to us, a family member, a lifelong friend, graduates from some sort of educational experience. Even the brother that calls you a knucklehead, will grudgingly say, "You did alright." But it is very different when you are the parent of the individual; watching your child walk across that stage. There is a strange mix of emotions ranging from sorrow, to pride, to joy. Sorrow because of all the years that have slipped through our fingers. Pride for all the dead ends, all the seemingly insurmountable obstacles, all the broken hearts along the way that were overcome to get to this moment. And joy; joy because this milestone is just one more step toward a fulfilling life of prosperity, success, and happiness that you just know they will experience.

But when the curtain of time lifted up on young nineteen-year-old William Hunter's path in the spring of 1555, it did not reveal awards of academic praise or notable standing among the faculty of an institution, indicating a prosperous future. No, William's parents watched as their son was not walked across a stage, but was escorted to the center of Brentwood, England where he was chained to a wooden post. They watched as he was then set ablaze. They stood by helplessly as their teenage son was burned at the stake.

- ∞☙ -

William Hunter, from an early age, was instructed in the teachings of the Reformation, which were in direct contrast to the teachings of the Catholic Church. William, no doubt, learned the three principal doctrines of the Reformation: Sola Scriptura (by Scripture alone); Sola Fide (by faith alone); and Sola Gratia (by grace alone). And it was through these bedrock truths, that saving faith entered the life of young William.

There is something so inspiring about youth. Beliefs are held so firmly and followed unwaveringly to their logical conclusion. Convictions have not suffered the slow chiseling of countless compromises made through the years. There is a stalwart, faithful stubbornness that comes with godly youth. That staunch stubbornness is probably what sparked the chain of events that led to the martyrdom of young William Hunter.

At the age of 19, William was sent to London, England to be a silk weaver's apprentice. While living there in the city home of the master silk weaver, a law was passed that required all people living in London to receive communion at the Easter Mass. Now there are some deep-seated theological reasons why William Hunter refused to observe this mass. Words like transubstantiation and consubstantiation enter into that reasoning and call for a lengthy explanation. But it will suffice to say that if William were to observe mass, it would be a rejection of the principal doctrines of his faith. So, he refused.

His refusal to obey the new Queen Mary's edict threw the master silk weaver into a panic. To ensure that he and his family were in no danger, the silk weaver forced William to move back to his hometown of Brentwood.

But that was not the end of his conflict with the religious world. His next run-in with the Catholic Church was several weeks later. Now, you and I have to understand that in 1555, Bibles were not found on every coffee table or on every nightstand. If there was a complete copy of the scriptures, it was kept, or most likely chained, to the pulpit of the local chapel. Not only were scriptures rare, but they were guarded. No one, save the local priest were allowed to even look at the Holy Bible. So it can easily be deduced that Williams next run-in with the Catholic Church was when he was discovered reading the Bible at the local chapel.

As he read, a Father Atwell, the local priest found him. "Are you meddling with the Bible? Do you know what you are reading? Can you expound the Scriptures?" Atwell said. The young man replied that he had no intention of expounding the Scriptures but was reading them for his own comfort. Father Atwell said, "It has not been a happy world since the Bible was circulated in English." Young William responded, "For God's sake, don't say that Father Atwell, for it is God's book from which we may learn what pleases and displeases God." "I know you!" Father Atwell said, "You're one of those who dislikes the Queen's laws. That's why you left

FORGOTTEN

London. If you don't mend your ways, you and many more heretics will broil, I promise you." "God give me grace that I may believe his Word and confess His name, whatever the consequences." was Williams reply.

From this point, the priest called the Vicar, and the Vicar called the local policeman, and the policemen had William delivered to the Bishop of London. William spent two days in the stocks, an incredibly painful public punishment. Then he was examined by Bishop Edmund Bonner of St. Paul's Cathedral, nicknamed "Bloody Bonner" because he burned more reformers than any other bishop.

Under the command of Bonner, William was locked up in prison and chained with as many chains as he would bear. Visiting his prison cell, Bonner asked him, "How old are you?" "Nineteen" "Well, you'll be burned before you're twenty if you don't do better than you did today!" William Hunter spent the next nine months in prison for his refusal to recant. On February 9, 1555, Bonner made his final offer to William. He resorted to bribery, promising money and employment if the teenager would only admit his 'errors.' William responded, "I thank you for your great offers, my Lord, but if you cannot persuade me from the Scriptures, I cannot turn from God for love of the world. I count all worldly things as loss and dung compared to the love of Christ." Bonner threatened, "If you die believing this way, you will be condemned forever." To which William responded, "God judges righteously, justifying those whom man condemns unjustly." And with those words, William sealed his fate.

WILLIAM HUNTER

It was just a few weeks later that William was sent to Newgate Prison in Brentwood to be executed before his family and friends. While there, we are told that Williams's parents visited him in prison, encouraging him to remain faithful, admitting their pride that their son was willing to die for Christ's sake. It was on March 26, 1555, that William Hunter was to be taken to the center of his hometown of Brentwood and burned at the stake.

Upon arriving at the stake, William knelt down and read the Fifty-first Psalm, until he came to these words, "The sacrifices of God are a broken spirit; a broken and a contrite heart, O God, Thou wilt not despise." When given one last opportunity to recant, William refused. He was bound to the stake, and a flame was kindled at his feet. Williams's brother, whose name is lost to history, cried out as the flames rose, "William, think on the holy passion of Christ, and be not afraid of death." "Behold," answered William, "I am not afraid." It was then that William Hunter lifted up his hands to heaven, and said, "Lord, Lord, Lord, receive my spirit." Then moments later, his head bowed in death as he was overcome by the smoke. And all the while, His parents watched. They looked on as their son graduated to glory.

We cannot begin to imagine what they felt at that moment. Some strange mix of emotions. Maybe a varying degree of sorrow, pride, and joy that other parents experience in those singular moments of accomplishment in the life of their children. Sorrow, a feeling of sadness like no other at the loss of their beloved son. Pride at the faithful testimony of their child. And maybe, just maybe, some small joy in that they will see their son again in that heavenly land.

FORGOTTEN

At the site of William's Martyrdom, there is a plaque that reads:

WILLIAM HUNTER. MARTYR. Committed to the Flames March 26, 1555. Christian Reader, learn from his example to value the privilege of an open Bible. And be careful to maintain it.

William Hunter believed that there was not only something worth living for but something worth dying for. William judged his life but a passing vapor compared to the preciousness of the Word of God and the testimony of Jesus Christ. William would agree with the Prophet Isaiah in the Old Testament and the Apostle Peter in the New Testament:

The grass withereth, the flower fadeth: but the word of our God shall stand for ever. (Isaiah 40:8, 1 Peter 1:24-25)

JOHN BROWN OF PRIESTHILL

There are few moments in life that fill the heart with joy and gladness like a wedding. One's wedding day is a time of happiness and contentment like none other. Yes, tears will be shed. But not all tears are testimonies to the sorrows of life. Such an occasion exudes an atmosphere of love in all of its many facets: A love like that of life-long friends and that of passionate lovers; a love that is selflessly giving and a love that is divinely descriptive.

It is also a symbol of hope. Hope for the days of long life to be shared between husband and wife. A wedding is all about the future. A groom vows to love and cherish from this day to the end of his life. The bride promises her undying love just the same. Each looks to the future with all the expectation in the world; just knowing that they will enter the twilight of their days with one hand clasp firmly in the others.

FORGOTTEN

All of the witnesses to the nuptial come by with their hugs and handshakes. They give their warmest words of love and affection, of admiration and advice. In nearly every case, they wish them many happy future years together. The pastor himself, the servant of God that performed the ceremony, may even give words of instruction as to guarding their marriage so that they might enjoy many years together.

But rare is the pastor who would tell the bride on her wedding day, "You have married a great man. Be sure to keep a death shroud close by because when you least expect it your husband is going to be killed." Even rarer still is the bride who would look at her bridegroom and know it to be true.

- ෩෬ -

John Brown was born in Scotland in 1627. By the time he came into manhood, he was surrounded by a very volatile and violent religious world. 100 years earlier, King Henry VIII decreed that England would break from the Catholic Church, forming what is called the Church of England. Simultaneously, in Scotland, a religious reformation, led by John Knox, instigated the formation of the Church of Scotland.

Now, there were varying degrees of difference between these two churches. The Church of England had a shadow of papal resemblance that did not sit well with the Church of Scotland. Also, the appointment of bishops and pastors was entirely at the will of the monarchy, not the local church. But one significant disagreement between these two churches was over the identity of the church's head.

JOHN BROWN OF PRIESTHILL

The Church of England decreed that the King of England was alone "the only Supreme Head in Earth of the Church." The Presbyterian doctrine of the Church of Scotland would have none of this. They held that the head of the church is Jesus Christ and Him alone. During the successive decades, a regal pressure was placed on Scotland to accept Church of England doctrine. In 1643, it became necessary for the Church of Scotland to outline their objections to conforming their religious practice. A document called the "Solemn League and Covenant" was drawn up. Scores of faithful Scottish Christians signed the document; many drawing blood from their own veins and using it as ink to solemnize the act. They became known as Covenanters.

The reaction of the throne of England to this dissent was violence. The years roughly from 1679 to 1688 were known as the "Killing Time." Covenanters were to be hunted, tortured, and executed by the thousands. Ministers were forced to flee for their lives into the hills and countrysides.

In the midst of these days, John Brown was a godly man that endeavored to eke out a life on a remote farm called Priesthill in Kyle, Ayrshire, just south of Glasgow. Somewhere in his early life, he had come to faith in Christ and had a sincere desire to serve the Lord, even in the midst of such difficult times. He received an education not from a school, but from these wandering outcast ministers, meeting in the hills and dales of seclusion.

Although he wanted to be a preacher, he was hampered and personally discouraged by some sort of speech impediment. Yet this was an impediment he was freed from when he went into prayer to God. He was said to have the gift to pour out his soul in prayer with eloquent language and great fervency. He also spent time teaching and training young people. With all the godly ministers, killed, or hiding under the threat of death, John, a simple layman, would gather young people from all around in his barn on Monday nights, and teach them the Word of God.

By the 1680s, John had already experienced much of the greatest joys and sorrows of life. John had taken a wife in the years prior. A wife that bare him, by some reports, a daughter named Janet and an infant son. But tragically, this first wife had passed away shortly after the birth of their son. History tells us nothing about this first wife or how she died. At this time in history, death lay very close to the surface of life. It was not coldly hidden away in a hospital or tucked away in a funeral home. Life was fragile, and the threat of death by disease or tragedy was a daily reality.

As soon as John recovered from the grief the death of his first wife, he became acquainted with Isabell Weir, from the parish of Sorn not too far from Priesthill. As far as personality goes, you could not ask for two more different people. John was reserve, grave and somewhat painfully shy, while Isabell was lively and cheerful. She could light up a room just by entering it. They two instantly fell in love, spending time with each other as John conducted business with her father.

The day finally came when John spoke to her concerning marriage. When he did so, he painted no rosy picture of what lay ahead for them if she should choose to marry him. He warned that one day he may be called upon to seal the Church's testimony with his blood. Isabell, bravely said, "If it should be so, through affliction and death, I will be your comfort. The Lord has promised me grace, and He will give you glory."

In 1682, exiled pastor and covenanter Alexander Pedan performed the wedding ceremony of John Brown and Isabell Weir in a secret location. During the illegal ceremony, Pedan said: "These witnesses of your vows have come at the risk of their lives to hear God's word and His ordinance of marriage." After the vows were exchanged and well-wishers were departing, Pedan pulled the bride aside and said, "You have got a good husband, value him highly, keep linen for a winding-sheet beside you, for in a day when you least expect it, thy master will be taken from thy head. In him, the image of our Lord and Saviour is too visible to pass unnoticed by those who drive the chariot wheels of persecution through the breadth and length of bleeding Scotland. But fear not, thou shalt be comforted." Just three years later, this haunting prophecy would come to pass.

John Graham, of Claverhouse, was a Scottish soldier and nobleman of some small degree. He was a Junior Lieutenant in the Scottish Army under the command of the Duke of Monmouth. When Claverhouse resigned his commission from the army, he returned to Scotland and was appointed captain by the King of England with orders to enforce the king's law which banned the gathering of Covenanters and to scour the countryside in search of them. One of the many men he set his sights on was John Brown of Priesthill. His reputation of piety and his unwillingness to conform to the religious demands of the king made him a target for Claverhouse.

FORGOTTEN

Early on the morning of May 1, 1685, John Brown arose before dawn to start the day's work on his farm. But not before he met with his God singing the first four verses of Psalm 27 "The LORD is my light and my salvation; whom shall I fear? the LORD is the strength of my life; of whom shall I be afraid? When the wicked, even my enemies and my foes, came upon me to eat up my flesh, they stumbled and fell. Though a host should encamp against me, my heart shall not fear: though war should rise against me, in this will I be confident. One thing have I desired of the LORD, that will I seek after; that I may dwell in the house of the LORD all the days of my life, to behold the beauty of the LORD, and to inquire in his temple."

His Bible reading, from John 16, was very fitting that morning. Its final words are Verse 33 in which Jesus said, "These things I have spoken unto you, that in me you might have peace. In the world you shall have tribulation: but be of good cheer; I have overcome the world." John then bowed his head in prayer. It is said that his morning prayer was as one, "lost to the world, and entered into the holy of holies, through the rent veil of the Redeemer's death."

Following that morning worship, John went into the neighboring hills of his land to prepare some peat-ground. It wasn't long before Claverhouse with three troops of dragoons surrounded him. They escorted him back to his home. As Brown bravely walked back to his house, Janet his daughter caught sight of a large number of horsemen being led by her father coming down the hill toward the house. She warned Isabell who said, "The thing that I feared is come upon me; give me grace for this hour!" She quickly wrapped John's baby son in a blanket and went outside to meet the assembly of soldiers.

JOHN BROWN OF PRIESTHILL

Claverhouse ordered the search of their home where covenanter literature was found. Claverhouse asked John why he had not been to the state-sanctioned church and if he would swear the oath of Abjuration (Now this is an oath that affirmed the divine right of the King as the head of the church). John Brown, who was plagued with a stammering speech, replied in a most precise and distinct voice, that he only acknowledged Christ Jesus as the head of the church. He added that he would not attend the state church because they were mere pawns of the King, and the only way he would obey and pray for the king is if he repented and turned from his wicked way.

Upon his response, Claverhouse exploded in fury, "Well then go to your prayers, for you shall immediately die." John Brown of Priesthill fell to his knees and began to call on God. He directed his prayers toward his wife, who was great with child, the babe in his arms and the daughter at her side. He prayed: "that every covenanted blessing might be poured upon her and her children, born and unborn, as one refreshed by the influence of the Holy Spirit, when He comes down like rain upon the mown grass, as showers upon the earth."

Claverhouse sneered and blasphemed interrupting his prayer twice. Finally, he had had enough and demanded that Brown rise from his knees. John Brown said to his wife, "Isabell, this is the day I told you of before we were married. You see me summoned to appear in a few minutes before the court of heaven, as a witness in our Redeemer's cause against the ruler of Scotland; are you willing that I should part from you?" No doubt through her sobs she yielded in obedience to God and replied "Heartily willing." John threw his arms around his family kissing them all good-bye.

FORGOTTEN

John then said, "That is all I wait for; death, where is thy sting? O grave, where will be thy victory? Blessed be thou, O Holy Spirit! that speaketh more comfort to my heart than the voice of my oppressors can speak terror to my ears!"

Claverhouse ordered six of his dragoons to shoot him. The men took aim, but the scene had so moved them to tears that they refused to fire. Claverhouse demanded that they fire their weapons, yet they still refused. Infuriated at their mutiny, Claverhouse dismounted his horse, drew his pistol from his belt, pressed the barrel to the head of Brown, and pulled the trigger.

A puff of blue smoke filled the air, with the acrid smell of burnt gunpowder. The shrill blast of the gun echoed off the nearby hills. Isabell and Janet screamed, and the baby cried. The bloody head of John Brown slumped over as his body crumpled to the ground. Claverhouse seized the moment to inflict as much pain on the grieving wife as he could. He asked, "What thinkest thou of thy fine husband now, woman?" Fixing her tear-filled gaze on Claverhouse, she said, "I ever thought much good of him, and more good than ever now." With a flash of violence in his eyes, he replied: "It were but justice to lay thee beside him." She replied, "If ye were permitted, I doubt not your cruelty could go that length; but how will ye answer for this morning's work." With an arrogant sneer, he said: "To men, I can be answerable, and as for God I will take Him in my own hands." And with that, he dug his spurs into his horse and rode away with his men.

JOHN BROWN OF PRIESTHILL

The poet Henry Inglis describes the moments that followed:

> *Tenderly, as on her marriage bed,*
> *The child on the moss she laid;*
> *And she stretched the cold limbs of the dead*
> *And drew the eyelids shade;*
> *And bound the corpse's Shattered head,*
> *And shrouded the martyr in his plaid*
> *And where the dead and the living slept*
> *Sat in the wilderness and wept.*

The few gleaming years that John and Isabell spent together were no doubt years of devotion and joy. Like other couples, they stayed up late into the night dreaming of a long future together. But always in the back of their minds, unspoken to the ear of each, was an awareness that all which is held dear in this world is fading and temporal. And that the world beyond this life, is the only one to truly prepare for.

As sweet as marital love is in the fleeting days of this life, it cannot be compared to the joys of that heavenly land. John Brown of Priesthill took to heart the words of the Lord Jesus when he said:

For whosoever will save his life shall lose it; but whosoever shall lose his life for my sake and the gospel's, the same shall save it. (Mark 8:35)

DR. ROWLAND TAYLOR

The word "minister" or "pastor" is a rather cheap identifier in society today. Any person with the slightest hint of religious inkling can stand up and declare themselves a spiritual leader. Even someone who wants to officiate a wedding can hop on the internet superhighway and stop off at any of a dozen ordination sites and for $34.99 can print off a certificate affirming them as a representative of God.

But deep down we all know that there is something more to this office or calling than a piece of paper. It's more than the vestments that they wear, the education they possess, the office they hold, or their eloquence of speech. Society may place a clergyman in a distinctive category simply by denominational affiliation, but that is not an accurate indicator that the minister is a divine ambassador.

FORGOTTEN

Some may measure the validity of a minister by the people that they lead. There are those that would look at the mega-church pastor and equate authenticity of his divine call by the enormous number that congregates each week to hear him. At the same time, there are others that believe just the opposite. The more sparse the spiritual leaders following and the less appealing his message is to the masses, the more he is seen as one who has not sold out to the lure of popularity; clearly affirming him as being the messenger of God.

But even these methods leave the weighing of a minister in the scales of fallible and faulty human perception. The only correct and clear measuring stick for a Christian leader is the word of God. In diverse places, and sparse wording, the Bible gives a sketch of a pastor. It lays out the character and the conditions for a pastor, along with its requirements and its responsibilities.

History has given us many examples of what it means to be a servant of God. Great men that have led dynamic movements, spoken to large crowds, written excellent books, and taken remarkable stands. But there are a select few that have paid for the privilege of leading the flock of God with their life's blood. Shepherds who have literally laid down their lives for their sheep. There is one, almost forgotten by history, who exhorted and encouraged his fold to be faithful to the word of God no matter what. Then sealed that testimony with his own blood.

- ಏಂಡ -

We are not privy to much of the early life of Roland Taylor. We know that he was born in Northumberland, the northernmost

DR. ROWLAND TAYLOR

county of England on October 6, 1510. We don't know anything of his conversion. He was born just before the era of the Reformation, and through the testimony of the latter days of his life, we know that he believed in salvation by grace through faith, the bedrock of Reformation teaching. We know something of his education. In 1530 he graduated from Cambridge University with a bachelor's degree in civil and canon law and in 1534 received his doctorate in the same discipline. After serving in varying roles, Dr. Taylor was presented to the church at Hadleigh, in Suffolk County, England and became their pastor in 1544. He would remain this church's pastor until his death in 1555.

The years of Roland Taylor's ministry were during a time of great political upheaval. In 1547 King Henry VIII died. His successor King Edward VI died in 1553. These two kings did much for the acceptance of Protestants in society. Their persecutions were limited during the reign of King Henry VIII, and King Edward VI abolished the requirement of clerical celibacy and the Catholic Mass. But with the death of King Edward VI and the ascension of Queen Mary I, all of these reforms were reversed. She wanted to reestablish Catholicism in England, vowing to weed out and burning every Protestant in England. And with this drastic change in political power, Roland Taylor found himself in the crosshairs of persecution.

Roland Taylor proved to be an excellent and beloved pastor to the people of Hadleigh. This town was about 70 miles outside of London, and not really a place for one to make a name for themselves. Author RC Ryle, while writing on Taylor, said, "If you want to be popular as a preacher, this is not where you serve." But serve there he did, in exemplary fashion.

FORGOTTEN

Whereas the practice of many in that time was to take the house and the farm that was given to support the minister, rent it out to farmers, and live a life entirely detached from the people of his charge, Dr. Taylor lived and served among the people of Hadleigh. One historian said, "He was a right and glorious image or pattern of all the qualities that Paul brings out in 1 Timothy 3 of a godly minister of Christ's church. He was the good salt of the earth. He was a light in God's house set upon a candlestick for all good men to imitate and follow." He had a fierce love for his flock and diligently instructed them through the faithful teaching of God's word. He would not let even the smallest gathering of his church disperse without teaching them some aspect of God's saving grace. He was also an approachable, gentle, and caring; giving to those in want; attending to the needs of the poor and the infirmed. Even when his enemies would insult him, he would return their scorn with words of love. And at the same time, he never shied away from stout rebuke to the rich and powerful who stood in need of correction. It was this love for the church that would initiate a conflict that would eventually lead to the taking of his life.

With the ascension of Queen Mary and her overturning of previous reforms in favor of Protestants, several people of Hadleigh saw it as their chance to reestablish Catholicism in the town. They went into the chapel at Hadleigh, and with a constructed alter and the necessary implements and garments began to conduct a Catholic Mass. This Catholic ceremony is a repudiation of the sufficiency of Christ, and it is an idolatrous practice. The men leading the Mass knew there would be opposition and set armed guards to prevent anyone from interfering with the ritual.

DR. ROWLAND TAYLOR

Roland Taylor heard the church bells ringing and assumed he was needed there. He arrived finding the doors of the chapel locked. Gaining entrance through the chancel door, he saw the men performing the mass surrounded by guards with drawn swords. Taylor shouted: "You devil! How do you dare enter this church of Christ and profane and defile it with this abominable idolatry?" One of the men said, "You traitor! Why are you disturbing the queen's proceedings?" "I'm not a traitor," Taylor responded, "I'm the shepherd of this flock, with every right to be here, I order you, you popish wolf – in the name of God, leave! Don't poison Christ's flock with your idolatry." It wasn't long before the guards forcibly escorted Dr. Taylor from the church.

This incident was quickly reported to Stephen Gardiner, the Bishop of Winchester. Gardiner sent a summons to Taylor, and despite the townspeople's desperate appeal for Taylor to flee, he boldly appeared before the Bishop. As soon as Taylor came before him, Gardiner lit into him with insults calling him basically a criminal, a traitor, and a heretic among other names. Dr. Taylor patiently withstood the abuse, then calmly responded, "My Lord, I am not a traitor or heretic, but a true subject and Christian. I came here at your command. Why did you send for me?" "Are you come a villain?" Gardiner sneered, "How dare you look me in the face? Don't you know who I am?" To which Taylor replied: "Yes. I know who you are. You are Dr. Stephen Gardiner, bishop of Winchester, and lord-chancellor and yet but a mortal man. But if I should be afraid of your lordly looks, why fear ye not God, the Lord of us all? You have forsaken the truth, denied our Saviour Jesus Christ and His word, and gone against your oaths. With what countenance will you appear before the judgment-seat of

Christ, and answer to your oath made first unto King Henry VIII, and afterward unto King Edward VI, his son?"

As you can imagine, these words did not sit well with the Bishop of Winchester. Roland spent the next two years in jail. During that time, there were so many protestant pastors and preachers committed into prison, that it took on a university atmosphere. Dr. Taylor spent much of his time over the following months praying, reading, and studying the scriptures.

Two years in chains; two years in deplorable conditions, two years with little food and yet this pastor's resolve was unbroken. He adamantly refused to relinquish the truth of God's word even though it would, in the end, cost him his life.

In early February 1555, Taylor was set to be transferred from London, back to Hadleigh. He was sent there to be executed before the very people that he loved and served as pastor. The night of his leaving London, he was allowed to secretly have dinner with his wife and children. As his wife, Margret departed, she knew he would be transferred sometime before morning. She and her two daughters hid outside the prison and waited until the wee hours of the morning, hoping to see him once more.

At 2am, Rowland appeared with the guards outside the prison. Elizabeth, their 13-year-old daughter, who they adopted when she was parentless at three, cried out, "O my dear father! Mother, mother, here is my father led away!" Margret then cried: "Rowland, Rowland, where art thou?" It was pitch black outside that night; no lanterns were lit during the prison transfer. Dr. Taylor responded, "Dear wife, I am here!" Margret came running

DR. ROWLAND TAYLOR

with Elizabeth and their younger daughter Mary. They crumpled to the ground in an embrace. The sheriff allowed them a few moments to say their goodbyes. There, kneeling on the ground, Rowland led them in the Lord's Prayer. As they stood, sobs could be heard from some of the guards and the sheriff. Rowland said to his no doubt tear-filled wife, "Farewell my dear wife, be of good comfort: for I am quiet in my conscience. God shall stir up a father for my children." He then kissed his daughter Mary and said: "God bless thee, and make thee His servant." Then he turned and kissing Elizabeth, he said: "God bless thee. I pray you all stand strong, and steadfast unto Christ, and His word, and keep you from idolatry."

In his last will and testament, Rowland further said to his wife and family: "The Lord gave you unto me, and the Lord hath taken me from you, and you from me: blessed be the name of the Lord! I believe that they are blessed which die in the Lord. God careth for sparrows, and for the hairs of our heads. I have ever found Him more faithful and favorable, than is any father or husband. Trust ye therefore in Him by the means of our dear Saviour Christ's merits: believe, love, fear, and obey Him: pray to Him, for He hath promised to help. Count me not dead, for I shall certainly live, and never die. I go before, and you shall follow after, to our long home."

The following night, as the company stayed at an inn called the Woolsack, Dr. Taylor's servant John Hull brought his young son Thomas to see him. The boy was seated on a horse next to Taylor as this Father lifted up his eyes to heaven and prayed for God's blessing on his son.

Over the next few days, as the detail traveled to Hadleigh, Dr. Taylor was joyful and happy. He readily engaged his guards endeavoring to convert them to Christ. When he was informed that they would be returning to Hadleigh, Rowland then prayed, "Oh good Lord, I thank thee that I shall yet once more before I die, see my flock whom Thou Lord knowest that I most heartily loved and truly taught. Good Lord, bless them and keep them steadfast in your word and in your truth." Before they arrived, Taylor's head was hooded, to obscure his face from the people that would begin to congregate at his arrival. As the company, rode into Hadleigh, although no one could see his face, many were sure it was their faithful pastor. The townspeople lined the streets weeping and crying for the fate of their pastor. One poor man and his five children came and knelt at the side of the road and prayed, "God help, and comfort thee, as thou hast many a time come to my aid, and helped my poor children!" Others cried out, "Ah good Lord, there goeth our good shepherd from us, that so faithfully hath taught us, so fatherly hath cared for us, and so godly hath governed us. O merciful God: what shall we poor scattered lambs do?"

During their route to the commons where he was to be executed, Taylor insisted that they stop at the almshouse, a place where the poorest of the poor found help. It was a site where Dr. Taylor's ministry had taken him many a time before. While there, Dr. Taylor took the remaining coins in his possession, given to sustain him in prison, placed them in a glove and tossed them through a window.

When they arrived at the commons, outside the church, Taylor was unsure as to where they were. When one of the guards told

DR. ROWLAND TAYLOR

him he was outside his parish church in Hadleigh, Taylor said, "Thanks be to God! I'm home!" It was then that the hood was removed and the crowd burst with emotion. His head had been notched and clipped to ridicule his appearance. But the crowd with sobs and tears began to encourage their pastor, "God save thee, good Dr. Taylor! Jesus Christ strengthen thee, and help thee! The Holy Ghost comfort thee!" In preparation for the burning, much of his clothing was removed. When he removed his boots, Taylor summoned a familiar face from the crowd and handed the boots to him; likewise with his coat and shirt. When he finished, he said to those gathered, "Good people, I have taught you nothing but God's holy Word, and those lessons I took out of the Holy Bible. Today I come to seal it with my blood." A guard, having enough of his talk, struck him on the head.

As he approached the stake, he knelt to pray, at which point a woman burst from the crowd to pray with her pastor. As she knelt down beside him, the guards tried to thrust her away, threatening to run her over with the horses. But she would not be moved. Finally, he arose from praying; he walked to the stake and there kissed it. After stepping into the pitch barrel they had provided for him, he folded his hands and with his eyes locked toward the heavens began to pray again. As he did so, an antagonist from the crowd threw a piece of wood at Taylor, striking him on the head and bloodying his face. Dr. Taylor responded to the injury by saying, "O friend, I have harm enough, what needed that?"

As Rowland Taylor stood, bound to the stake, he began to recite the 51st Psalm. For this, he was struck on the mouth and demanded to quote the scripture in Latin. A fire was then kindled at his feet. Dr. Taylor lifting up both hands toward heaven, called

FORGOTTEN

upon God saying, "Merciful Father of heaven! For Jesus Christ, my Saviour's sake, receive my soul into thy hands!" It was then, one of the guards, either out of malice or mercy, struck Rowland Taylor on the head with a halberd, a long ax type weapon, crushing his skull and killing him instantly. His body went limp and fell over into the flames that grew higher and higher. And yet, in the exact same moment, his soul and spirit were received into glory, no doubt to the words, "Well done thou good and faithful servant."

As with so many others of the Christian faith, there is little left to stir the memory of this faithful pastor. He wrote no books. His sermons are lost to time. No school bears his name. A barely legible marker, obscured by tall weeds, placed at the location of his death stands as a record of his memory. He is all but nearly forgotten.

But what we do have of him is enough to produce a benchmark, a measuring stick for any would be pastor or minister. The boldness of his conviction and his unwavering obedience to revealed truth are desperately in short supply when compared to the relativistic situational ethic of the present. And yet this was tempered with an earnest love and gentle humility, making him a Christ-like example for any generation. He is one indeed that walks in the footsteps of the Lord Jesus, one that:

...giveth his life for the sheep. (John 10:11)

MARGARET WILSON

Marina Keegan, a 22-year-old Yale graduate, wrote in her journal, "We don't have a word for the opposite of loneliness, but if we did, I could say that's what I want in life." She wrote these words before her life was cut short by a tragic car accident in May of 2012. The essence of such wise words from a young person so suddenly taken in death, bring to the surface a human need that we all have: The need to belong. The opposite of loneliness is a sense of belonging.

We are conditioned in the earliest moments of life with a need for belonging. In most circumstances, as soon as we are born into this world, we belong. We belong to a mother. We belong to a father. We belong to a family. We belong to a community. And with that belonging comes a feeling of safety and security; a sense of one's place in the world.

FORGOTTEN

As we grow, we search for ever-widening circles of belonging. We find ourselves striving to fit in and be accepted by our peers. The driving reason for this is the need to belong. We search for belonging in career choices and civic organizations. We look for that same sense of belonging in a marriage.

But life has a way of chipping away at that feeling of belonging. Separations and broken relationships tend to alienate us; causing us to lose hold on the reality of our belonging. Betrayals and failures, although a part of every person's life, leave us isolated and alone. And that's really what we all fear; doing life alone; venturing out with no one by our side. It is entirely natural to think that we forfeit the sense of belonging when we go it on our own.

But that was not the case with an eighteen-year-old Scottish girl by the name of Margaret Wilson. She had taken a lonely road for most of her formative years; living in wilderness caves, trying merely to survive when she was only in her teenage years. And all that time, she never lost sight of her belonging. Even in the final moments of her life, when it seemed that all the world was against her, she spent the last breaths of her body boldly affirming that she belonged to only One.

- ෴ -

By the early 17th century, England and Scotland had joined the Reformation, departing from Catholicism. However, that did not mean they were both cut from the same cloth. 100 years earlier, King Henry VIII decreed that England would break from the Catholic Church. However, in doing so, he ordered that he alone be "the only Supreme Head in Earth of the Church of England." On the other hand, the Reformation in Scotland was led by John Knox. Now, much could be said concerning this giant of the reformation and the rise of Presbyterianism in Scotland. He wielded a power in Scotland that rivaled the very monarchy. Mary Queen of Scots is reputed to have said: "I fear the prayers of John Knox more than all the assembled armies of Europe." But one thing is for sure, despite all of his power in the church and the affairs of the nation of Scotland, John Knox was clear in his teaching that the head of the church is Jesus Christ and Him alone.

There were other points of contention between the Church of England and the Presbyterian Church of Scotland, to be sure. The Church of England had a shadow of papal resemblance that did not sit well with the Church of Scotland. Also, the appointment of bishops and pastors was utterly at the will of the monarchy, not the local church. John Knox had laid a doctrinal foundation from the Bible that would not yield room for the Church of England, and that foundation held strong long after the death of Knox in 1572.

But over the successive decades, the regal pressure was placed on Scotland to accept Church of England doctrine. In 1643, it became necessary for the Church of Scotland to outline their objections to being forced into conforming their religious practice. A document called the Solemn League, and Covenant was drawn up. Scores of faithful Scottish Christians signed the document; many drawing blood from their veins and using it as ink to solemnize the act.

FORGOTTEN

During the successive reigns of Kings Charles II and James VII in the mid to late 1600s, the pressure to conform to Church of England practice, thereby bowing to the King of England, became violent. The years roughly from 1679 to 1688 were known as the "Killing Time." Signers of the "Solemn League and Covenant" known as Covenanters began to be hunted, tortured and executed. As many as 18,000 Christians who would not compromise their beliefs suffered persecution. Covenanters were forced to run into the hills and country-sides to hide. They would meet in secret open-air meetings called conventicles. Every time they would meet, they ran the risk of being caught and imprisoned, banished from the country, or even executed. Blood-thirsty members of the British army would scour the countryside looking for rebels. Any person that failed to attend the Church of England services would be fined and suspected of being a rebel; opening themselves up to harsh questioning, even under the pains of torture. Upon suspicion of being a Covenanter, a person would often be asked to declare the Oath of Abjuration; a statement renouncing the "Solemn League and Covenant" and swearing allegiance to the Crown of England as the head of the church.

In 1667, during this heated time of religious oppression Gilbert Wilson, a farmer of modest means in Glenvernoch, Parish of Penninghame, Scotland, became the father to a daughter named Margaret. In all, he would have five sons and two daughters and do his best to avoid any conflict in such volatile days. Gilbert Wilson and his wife were dutiful members of the Church of England; willingly surrendering their doctrinal beliefs to avoid trouble. But his sons and daughters refused to yield what they knew to be true from the word of God, choosing instead to suffer

MARGARET WILSON

the consequences. History tells us that in 1684, an 18-year-old Margaret, her brother of 16 years Thomas and he sister Agnus age 13, fled from their home into the nearby hills to hide from British troops. There they would take cover in caves and huts, doing whatever they could to survive.

In February 1685, King Charles died and the new King, James ascended the throne. With this change in power, it looked as though there might be a relaxing of the persecutions aimed at non-conformists. In the mind of Margret and her siblings, it seemed to be an excellent time to be reunited with fellow believers. Leaving behind their hiding places, Margret and Agnes went down into Wigstown to visit with friends, particularly an elderly widow Margaret McLachlan. While they were there, they were all betrayed by a local man who reported their presence to the authorities. It was then that the two Wilson girls, along with the elderly Margaret, were taken prisoner. Once taken prisoner under suspicion of being a Covenanter, they were asked to make the Oath of Abjuration, to which they all refused.

They were brought to trial on April 13th, 1685, and the court proceedings were a farce. During the trial, the girls were accused of participating in the Battle of Bothwell Bridge, a skirmish between British troops and Covenanter forces that took place when the girls were only small children. In the end, all three were sentenced to be tied to posts that were fixed in the sand, within the flood mark, at the mouth of the Blednoch River, and there to stand till the floodwaters flowed over them, and [they] drowned." Gilbert Wilson, unwilling to yield quietly to the execution of his beloved daughters, sold all his possessions of any value, borrowed from relatives and neighbors, managing to raise about a hundred pounds, which was an enormous sum at the time. He rode to Edinburgh to buy his daughters' pardon. He was only able to acquire the release of one, Agnes, his youngest child.

On May 11, 1685, Margaret Wilson, along with Margaret McLachlan were taken to Blednoch River, a tributary of the Irish Sea in the North Atlantic to have their executions carried out. The two women were separated by some distance. The elder Margaret was taken closer to the advancing tide so the younger Margaret would watch her friend die, in hopes that it would cause her to recant. With each wave, Margaret Wilson saw the waters mounting higher and higher; from McLachlan's knee, to her waist, to her neck and chin, and finally her lip. In the end, she watched as her friend sank entirely into the salty waters of the tide.

But what was supposed to strike terror in the heart of the young woman had the opposite effect. When a heartless bystander, possibly one of the soldiers, asked young Margaret what she thought of watching her friend die, she replied, "What do I see, but Christ, in one of His members, wrestling there. Think you that we are the sufferers? No, it is Christ in us; for He sends none a warfare upon their own charges."

As the tide slowly rose around the body of young Margaret, eyewitnesses testified that she began to sing the 25th Psalm starting at verse seven, "Remember not the sins of my youth, nor my transgressions: according to thy mercy remember thou me for thy goodness' sake, O LORD. Good and upright is the LORD: therefore will he teach sinners in the way."

MARGARET WILSON

Her executioners allowed her hands to be free, binding only her waist to the stake in the waters. In her hand was a Bible from which she read aloud. The cold waters of the Atlantic echoed with her angelic voice as she read from Romans chapter 8: "Who shall separate us from the love of Christ? shall tribulation, or distress, or persecution, or famine, or nakedness, or peril, or sword? As it is written, For thy sake we are killed all the day long; we are accounted as sheep for the slaughter. Nay, in all these things we are more than conquerors through him that loved us. For I am persuaded, that neither death, nor life, nor angels, nor principalities, nor powers, nor things present, nor things to come, Nor height, nor depth, nor any other creature, shall be able to separate us from the love of God, which is in Christ Jesus our Lord."

Moments later, the waters reached her lips, and she began to struggle. The detail of soldiers overseeing the execution was commanded to go out to her and give her one more chance to relent. The guards loosened the ropes enough to lift her head above water. "Pray for the King for he is supreme over all persons in the church," they said. With gentleness in her voice, she replied, "I wish the salvation of all men and the damnation of none." The frustrated soldiers thrust her head back under the waters. Drawing her back up, they demanded, "Pray for the King! Swear the oath!" A broken-hearted spectator nearby cried out to the young girl, "Dear Margaret, say, 'God save the king!' Say, 'God save the king!'" Margret responded, "Lord, give the king repentance, forgiveness, and salvation if it be Thy holy will." Her watching supporters suddenly pleaded with the authorities over the execution, "Sir, she has said it! She has said it!" But they were not satisfied. It was demanded that she should swear the oath of abjuration, or be lowered into the sea never to return.

At that moment, life hung in the balance, she was alone, more alone than any human being could be. With her face pale, and lips turning to blue she said these words, "I will not; I am one of Christ's children; let me go."

With a sneer in his voice, a soldier forced her underneath the water saying, "Take another drink." And moments later Margaret's lifeless body swayed with the ebb and flow of the evening tide.

There are countless instances in life where we will be alone; where we will be void of that sense of belonging; moments where we will have to do life with no one at our side; times when it seems like all the world is against us. It is in those moments where we must find that our experience of belonging need not end when the last person we know turns their back and walks away. Through the One who not only overcame life, but defeated death, and reigns supreme in the heavens, we can belong; belong in such a way so as to never really be alone, to always know the security and safety of being the treasured possession of the living Christ. Through Him, we can say along with Margaret Wilson,

I am my beloved's, and my beloved is mine... (Song of Solomon 6:3)

JAMES ABBES

When John Foxe compiled his book entitled the Acts and Monuments, which would later become known as Foxe's Book of Martyrs, it was the first of its kind: A single volume with the sole purpose of bringing together the numerous accounts of Christians who gave their lives because of their faith in Jesus Christ. Such a volume had never been compiled. Witnesses to Foxe's endeavor testified that he persisted in maintaining the highest standard of honesty in his findings and that he was a "sincere seeker after truth."

Although history, actual historical events, cannot wash away the truth, it can obscure it. Eyewitnesses pass away in death before their testimonies are ever recorded. Sometimes when those accounts are penned, they are lost or destroyed by elements of time.

FORGOTTEN

Such is the case with James Abbes. There is very little available to an enquirer save John Foxe's account; an account, which compared to others, is not much more than a footnote. We know nothing of his origin, the date of his birth, the role he played in the Christian church or the Reformation as a whole. He is described as a young man, with a zeal to share the message that the monarchy desperately longed to stamp out: The plain teaching of salvation by grace through faith in Jesus alone. This teaching was considered heresy and punishable by death and in 1555, the list was long and growing of those who were paying the ultimate price for their faith in Jesus alone.

- ℘◯℘ -

Something that James Abbes was doing, whether it was preaching, or teaching, or evangelizing, caught the attention of the authorities and an order for his arrest was issued by the bishop of Norwich. Abbes wandered from place to place, like a fugitive, looking for a place to hide from apprehension among brethren. But somewhere among these supposed friends, was a betrayer. One who informed the authorities as to his whereabouts and James Abbes was arrested.

He was brought before the Bishop of Norwich, a man named John Hopton. The Bishop was set on causing this young man to recant his beliefs. He went at young Abbes with the most frightening of threats. The means of execution varied considerably during this time from burning at the stake; to being drawn and quartered (dismembered); and being beheaded, just to name a few. No doubt, Bishop Hopton used these threats to their full extent.

JAMES ABBES

After these threats of brutal torture were seemingly ineffective, the bishop then began to lighten his tone. He spoke to James with enticing speech, imploring the young man to be sensible and reasonable, minimizing the magnitude of a simple change of heart, and salting his offer with the promise of money, and finally, the Bishop got his way. The bold, fugitive of faith, James Abbes, recanted his belief. He was immediately freed, carrying with him the sum of twenty or forty pence in his hand.

As the young man began his journey home a free man, all the reasoning and posturing of the Bishop's arguments began to wear off. With every step, conviction of soul set in. The coins in his pocket cease to be 20 or 40 pence but felt heavy with the weight of 30 pieces of silver. The echo of his voice stating the denial of what he knew to be the truth, sounded more and more like the words of a disciple saying, "I know not the man!" At that moment, every bird sounded like a cock crowing. He could sense the eyes of the Lord Jesus looking at him as the denier that he had become.

It was then he realized the significance of what he had just done. And somewhere on the road, with his heart throbbing with anticipation, he did an about-face and headed back to stand before the Bishop of Norwich. He knew what this would mean; the bishop would not be happy with this sudden change of heart. But James could not take another step down the road of betrayal.

Upon arriving, he threw the money down at the Bishop's feet, reclaiming his conviction; repenting that he had ever yielded to their wicked persuasion. Although he was like Peter in his denial, he also mirrored his contrition and his later boldness. The Bishop and his chaplains tried to win him over again, to no avail. And in the end, his courage was rewarded with a sentence to be burned at the stake.

On August 2, 1555, James Abbes was carried to Bury, England to suffer his execution. When he arrived, he was commanded to undress. James handed his clothes to the needy around him. Where he was going, he had a brand new robe awaiting him. As he was taken to the execution site, bound to the stake and the wood prepared around him, he consistently exhorted the spectators to steadfastly cling to the truth of God's word and Christ as their only means of salvation, even if it means that they too seal their testimony with their own blood. It was then that one of the Sheriff's servants began to mock him and blaspheme, calling Abbes a heretic and a lunatic.

James Abbes was positioned and secured among the wood then the flame was kindled. As the fire rose around Abbes, the Sheriff's servant that mocked him earlier began to act erratically, as if he were mad. He began to take off his clothes as James did moments before while saying "Thus did James Abbes, the true servant of God, who is saved, but I am damned." He repeated this phrase over and over, growing more and more agitated until finally, the Sheriff had him secured, tied to a cart, and delivered to his master's home.

Once home, still struck with such madness, his master had him bound and kept in the dark room in hopes that he would regain his senses. But from within that room, one could hear the statement over and over: "James Abbes was a true servant of God, who is saved, but I am damned." It was not six months later that this man was taken in death.

JAMES ABBES

James Abbes was burned at the stake that August day in 1555, joining in a long list of others who would meet the same fate for their stand on the truth of the gospel of Jesus Christ. But these final moments in the life and death of Abbes send a clear message to us. A message not only about the necessity of being faithful to Jesus no matter what. But also of the reality of our own frailty. There are pressures and distresses in life that can cause us to stumble and fall, to even deny the Lord that saved us. There are times when we, by our actions, deny the Lord as loudly as Peter or Abbes did. We all make regrettable decisions.

But James Abbes shows us that it's never wrong to go back and make it right; to face our betrayal with honesty and repentance; to go back to the point of failure and retake our stand for Jesus, no matter what. Because the word of God assures us that,

...if we confess our sins, he is faithful and just to forgive us our sins, and to cleanse us from all unrighteousness. (1 John 1:9)

MAEYKEN WENS

In his well-known sermon that he preached over twelve hundred times during his ministry, the famed pastor R.G. Lee said this about women, "...the spiritual life of a nation, city, town, school, church, or home never rises any higher than the spiritual life of women. When women sag morally and spiritually, men sag morally and spiritually. When women slump morally and spiritually, men slip morally and spiritually."

He then went on to say that the converse was true as well: "But while that is true, it is also gloriously true that some of the most beautiful and spiritually fragrant flowers that blossom in God's Kingdom gardens, some of the most luscious spiritual fruit that ripens in God's Kingdom orchards and some of the most potent streams that flow out to make gardens out of desert spots of the world are realities because of woman's chastity, faith, service, sacrifice, and devotion."

FORGOTTEN

If this is so, then in the garden of the history of the Christian church, tucked in an out of the way corner is a beautiful rose that is the life of Maeyken Wens.

— ⁂ —

Although many attempted to make known the truth of the gospel of Jesus Christ, for centuries it had been covered over by the superstition and tradition of the Catholic Church. It was not until 1517 and the nailing of the Ninety-five Theses to the church house door at Whittenburg, Germany by a Catholic monk by the name of Martin Luther, that a wave of change was unleashed that could not be stamped out by the established church. This illuminating change, this message of the grace of God to be had solely through the person and work of Jesus Christ, quickly spread throughout Europe. It caused many to look at the scriptures through fresh eyes and come to conclusions which were radically different from the practice of the Catholic Church.

One such group were the Anabaptist. The Catholic and Protestant tradition was that baptism was performed not long after birth. This practice was deeply entrenched not only in church tradition but in the state as well. Recognition as a citizen came from this church rite performed on the infant.

But as believers in Christ looked carefully at the scriptures, many became convinced that the ordinance of baptism was to be experienced by those who have consciously and intentionally placed their faith and trust in Jesus Christ. The religious world around them watched in shock as they followed the New Testament example, going into the waters of baptism as an adult.

MAEYKEN WENS

They were derided and scorned being called Anabaptist, or again baptizers. This name stuck and with it came an onslaught of fierce persecution.

Maeyken Wens lived during the mid-16th century. She was the wife of Mattheus Wen who by trade was a stone mason, but by the call of God was an Anabaptist pastor in Antwerp, Belgium. Such a calling was dangerous for one never knew when the practice of their out-lawed faith would cost them their lives. Yet in the spring of 1573, it was not Mattheus who would pay the price for his deeply held conviction, but his precious wife, Maeyken.

She along with several other women were discovered exercising their faith in a meeting of prayer and Bible study, merely worshiping God by the dictates of their conscience. They were arrested and imprisoned. Catholic authorities knew that this was an opportunity to make an example using the soft spot of their women to inflict maximum pain upon those practicing what they deemed as heretical teaching. From April to October of 1573, these women were tortured, cruelly abused, and subjected to constant badgering and intimidation in hopes that they would renounce their beliefs and embrace Catholic dogma. For seven long months, these women would be deprived of their families and live in the deplorable conditions of a mid-evil prison cell.

All that remains of this experience are a handful of letters that Maeyken Wens wrote to her husband and nine children. These letters reveal a woman of real tangible vulnerabilities coupled with a spiritual strength in Christ Jesus. To her husband, she wrote of her difficulty with enduring persecution with a thankful heart, "I regret, that I am not more thankful for all that comes upon me, for it is all the work of the Lord. We ought to thank the Lord in adversity as well as in that which is agreeable to the flesh; for if the Lord takes all from us, He takes from us no more than what He has lent us, for it belongs to us no longer than it pleases the Lord, Oh that I could always thank the Lord as well when the flesh suffers adversity, as when it prospers then we can thank the Lord indeed. ...O my very dear and beloved husband, pray the Lord heartily in my behalf, to remove the conflict from me; for it is in His power, if it is His pleasure. Truly the Lord has said, He that does not forsake everything is not worthy of me; for the Lord well knew that it would come hard to the flesh. But I hope that the Lord will also help me through even as He has helped many, and for which I can simply trust Him."

Maeyken was selflessly concerned for the financial well-being of her family when it came to the subject of visiting her in prison writing to her husband, "As regards further the visiting, you may do in the matter according to your pleasure; for I should indeed often desire your visit, were it not for the expense. But if you want to make your heart glad, you may come; I dare say nothing else, except that it costs so much, else I should desire to have you come soon. If you come, go to no expense in the way of bringing anything with you, as it costs far too much."

Her deep love for her husband and the pain of heart-rending separation can be felt in these words, "O my dear friend, I should never have thought that parting should come so hard to me as it does. True the imprisonment seemed hard to me, but that was because they were so tyrannical, but now the parting is the hardest of all."

MAEYKEN WENS

In a later letter to her husband, her resolve in the Lord is found to be unshaken saying, "Beloved husband and brother in the Lord, I inform you that my heart is still fixed to offer up a sacrifice to the Lord, the Lord be praised for the great grace which He shows to me poor, miserable creature. And I am also tolerably well according to the flesh, as I trust through the grace of the Lord that it is also with you, my most beloved in the Lord. Nothing more for this time, but I commend you to the Lord and to the words of His grace; this is the good wish and greeting of my heart. Farewell. Pray for me. By me, your dear wife and sister in the Lord. Maeyken Wens"

Some of the most stirring words from the pen of Maeyken were written to her firstborn son Adriaen, who she pleaded with to follow the Lord:

"My dear child Adriaen, my son, I leave you this for a testament, because you are the oldest, to exhort you that you should begin to fear our dear Lord, for you are getting old enough to perceive what is good or evil...My son, from your youth, follow that which is good and depart from evil do good while you have time, and look at your father, how lovingly he went before me with kindness and courteousness, always instructing me with the Word of the Lord..."

"Hence, my dear son; beware of that which is evil, that you will not have to lament afterward... Hear the instruction of your mother hate everything that is loved by the world and your sensuality, and love God's commandment, and let the same instruct you, for it teaches, If any man will come after me, let him deny himself, that is, forsake his own wisdom, and pray, Lord, thy will be done. If you do this, the anointing of the Holy Ghost will teach you all that you are to believe. Believe not what men say, but obey that which the New Testament commands you, and ask God to teach you His will. Trust not in your understanding, but in the Lord, and let your counsel abide in Him, and ask Him to direct you into His ways."

"My child, learn how you are to love God the Lord, how you are to honor your father and all other commandments which the Lord requires of you. Whatsoever is not contained therein, believe not; but whatever is contained therein, obey. Join yourself to those that fear the Lord, and depart from evil, and through love do all that is good..."

"My dear son, yield yourself to that which is good; the Lord will give you understanding. I give you this as my last adieu to you. My dear child, heed the Lord's chastening; for whenever you do evil, He will chasten you in your mind; desist, then, and call to the Lord for help, and hate that which is evil, and the Lord will deliver you, and good will come to you."

On the eve of her execution, just after she was sentenced to be burned at the stake, she wrote to her son Adrian again saying, "O my dear son, though I am taken from you here, strive from your youth to fear God, and you shall have your mother again up yonder in the New Jerusalem, where parting will be no more. My dear son, I hope now to go before you; follow me thus as much as you value your soul, for besides this there shall be found no other way to salvation."

MAEYKEN WENS

"Thus, I will now commend you to the Lord; may He keep you. I trust the Lord that He will do it if you seek Him. Love one another all the days of your life; take Hansken on your arm now and then for me. And if your father should be taken from you, care for one another. The Lord keep you one and all. My dear children, kiss one another once for me, for remembrance. Adieu, my dear children, all of you. My dear son, be not afraid of this suffering; it is nothing compared to that which shall endure forever. The Lord takes away all fear; I did not know what to do for joy when I was sentenced. Hence cease not, to fear God, because of this temporal death; I cannot fully thank my God for the great grace which He has shown me."

"Adieu once more, my dear son Adriaen; ever be kind, I pray you, to your afflicted father all the days of your life, and do not grieve him; this I pray all of you, for what I write to the oldest, I also mean to say to the youngest. Herewith I will commend you to the Lord once more. I have written this, after I was sentenced, to die for the testimony of Jesus Christ, on the fifth day of October, in the year of our Lord Jesus Christ, 1573."

On the morning of October 6, Maeyken Wens, along with the other women taken captive with her whose names are lost to history, were brought forth from their prison of confinement to be publicly burned at the stake. It did not take long for the Catholic Church to realize the power within the final words executed heretics; who surprisingly did not beg for their lives screaming in agony, but on the whole held fast to their confession by seemingly supernatural means. The dying words and exhortations of martyrs had a profound effect on the witnesses to the execution. Instead of acting as a warning and a deterrent to anyone who would oppose the teaching of the church, they became an accelerant igniting the passion of many to place their faith and trust in Jesus Christ alone.

To stay this effect, the Catholic Church devised a technique to silence its victims. The tongue screw was a device designed with two small iron tongs that could be used to reach in and pinch the tongue pulling it out of the mouth. The apparatus was fitted with a screw that threaded through the tong then into and through the tongue. Once affixed, the bulky device hanging outside of the mouth would prevent the individual from uttering one intelligible word.

Moments before her execution, this device was clasped to the tongue of Maeyken Wens so that not one song of praise to God could be sounded from her lips, not one prayer of thanksgiving could be heard, not one word of testimony could be shared before the gawking eyes of the execution witnesses. In silence, she, along with her companions were marched out to the prepared stakes, the charges against them read, and their bodies were set ablaze.

Among the eyes of witnesses was her beloved 15-year-old son Adriaen, who could not stay away from the execution of his precious and faithful mother. With his three-year-old brother Hans in his arms, he was determined to get one last glimpse of the one who brought him into this world and who was willing to spare no expense to bear witness of the one who gave His all on the cross for her. But as his mother was brought out and bound to the stake, Adriaen was so overcome with emotion at the scene before him and the trauma so great to his heart that he lost consciousness.

MAEYKEN WENS

By the time he awoke, the fires of execution had consumed the body of his mother and reduced her to charred remains of blackened ash and bones. With the stench of burnt flesh weighing heavy in the air, Adriaen dragged himself over the stake where his mother once stood. No doubt through tear-filled eyes, he probed the darkened ash heap for the only impervious reminiscence of his mother's faithfulness, the tongue screw. The torturous device that held her silent would be the memorial by which her love and devotion to Jesus Christ would forever be known.

In the letter to her husband, where she lamented her inability to be thankful for the suffering she was given to endure, Maeyken Wens wrote the following: "Oh, how easy it is to be a Christian, so long as the flesh is not put to the trial, or nothing has to be relinquished; then it is an easy thing to be a Christian."

In a day of casual Christianity, where the cost of following Christ seems to be held as a closely guarded secret so as not to frighten away the curious inquirer that might sit in a pew for a passing moment and drop a few paltry coins in the coffer; the words of this faithful pastor's wife may sound odd or maybe even unchristian. But the message of Jesus is explicit in its call. In order to walk in His steps, we must deny ourselves; we must surrender to our own cross; we must value the unseen and the eternal over the invites of this present and pleasurable world.

Maeyken Wens displayed this in her martyrdom; a disregard for the suffering being inflicted by her tormentors and a focus on that celestial object which can never be taken away. Jesus brought this mindset into sharp focus when he said,

FORGOTTEN

…Be not afraid of them that kill the body, and after that have no more that they can do. But I will forewarn you whom ye shall fear: Fear him, which after he hath killed hath power to cast into hell; yea, I say unto you, Fear him. (Luke 12:4-5)

MARINUS OF CAESAREA

One may not remember much from their required educational studies of the American poets. Names like Longfellow, Whitman, Poe, and Dickenson may ring a bell but few, if any, could recall a line or two. However, if you were questioned as to the meaning of the phrase "the road less traveled" you could probably identify it as something that came from a poem. You may not remember the author or even the title of the poem, but more than likely you will know how the poem ends:

Two roads diverged in a wood,

And I − I took the one less traveled by,

And that has made all the difference.

The name of the poem is "The Road Not Taken," and the author is Robert Frost. Down through the years, many people have debated the actual message that Frost was trying to communicate through the poem. Some see it as the value for free thinking and personal self-expression apart from the crowd. On the other hand, many who are more familiar with Robert Frost's work will say that he was pointing out the indecision people show with genuinely inconsequential decisions.

Now when it comes to a poem, we must never forget the old adage, "Beauty is in the eyes of the beholder." You may see this poem in either fashion; you may perceive meaning on whichever side of the argument, or you could have your own entirely different interpretation. That's fine. But what you cannot deny is that on this road of life, that Frost so eloquently describes, an inevitable choice has to be made; a destiny has to be determined; a path has to be taken.

For every one of us, life is filled with choices, some more significant than others, but decisions that nevertheless have to be made. However, no choice in life is more paramount than what is set forth in the claims of the Christian faith. The truth of the Bible reveals that there two roads; two ways; two destinies. Destinies that are infinitely separated apart. Whereas many views of the world can seemingly allow for an individual to walk down both paths; all paths; or every path; faith in Jesus Christ demands that one make a choice. Down through the centuries, many people have made this difficult choice, but few so brilliantly reveal the cost of following Christ like that of a young Roman soldier named Marinus of Caesarea.

MARINUS OF CAESAREA

Valerian became the Emperor of Rome around the beginning of the 3rd century. He singled out Christianity as a threat to the Roman Empire and through a series of edicts tried to stamp it out. Christian clergy were forced to perform sacrifices to the Roman gods or face banishment and eventually execution. Many Christians had their properties seized and were reduced to slavery. When Valerian's son Gallienus became Emperor in AD 260, all of these laws were rescinded, and toleration was extended to the followers of the Way. However, that was not the case for members of the Roman army. Although in the early fourth century, Constantine would cause the soldiers of the Roman Army to march into battle under the sign of the Christian Cross that was not the case in 263 AD. In the Roman Army, religions outside the polytheistic Roman system were seen as being incompatible with allegiance to Rome. Soldiers who would not perform the customary sacrifice to the Emperor of Rome would be subject to execution.

In his writings, Eusebius, the noted Greek historian, briefly recorded the story of a Roman soldier that was confronted with this issue. Marinus of Caesarea was from a highly regarded and wealthy family in Palestine. He was also a devoted Roman soldier who proved to be exceptionally valued. He was a decorated and highly esteemed infantryman. When his commanding officer, through death, had vacated the position of a Centurion, Marinus was in line to be promoted in rank.

But when he was brought before a military tribunal to be granted commission, another soldier came in before the tribunal and halted the proceedings. Because of his envy for the position, he charged that the promotion was not legal; that according to the ancient Roman law he could not be given the honor. He then followed with the accusation that Marinus was a Christian and therefore would not sacrifice to the emperor. All eyes were then fixed on Marinus. What was once the most exciting moment in his life, had suddenly become one of the tensest.

The tribunal judge, Achaeus, then asked Marinus to respond to the charge: Are you a Christian? With a thousand thoughts invading his mind all at once, seconds seemed like hours. The pounding heart within his breast could be felt all over his body. Before he knew it, he had suddenly affirmed that he was indeed a Christian. When asked to clarify his answer, Marinus again confessed to the tribunal that he was a follower of the religion that was so incompatible with Roman culture. Judge Achaeus looked the young soldier up and down, the silence of his deliberation was heavy in the air. All could see what was going on. They could see the envy of this indictment; and that this was just a ploy to deprive an obviously noble and deserving soldier his due. However, the law is the law. Judge Achaeus, not wanting to lose such an excellent soldier, decided to give Marinus three hours to reconsider his response.

Eusebius records that as Marinus left the tribunal, he was met by Theotecnus, the Bishop of Caesarea. No doubt his pastor, Theotecnus began to speak words of encouragement into the young soldier's ear as he led him into the church. However, he could see the decision weighed heavily on the mind of Marinus. This answer was not about admiration or embarrassment. It was not about demotion or commission. This answer was about life and death. The intended result of the three-hour respite from Judge Achaeus was coming to pass. The battle within this soldier's heart was raging high. The question kept ringing in the mind of Marinus, "What path should I choose? What road do I take?"

Finally, the wise Bishop realized how to make the answer clear. Theotecnus left the room to retrieve one of the sacred scrolls of copied scripture. Then Theotecnus motioned for the soldier's sword that rested at his side. Marinus handed him the weapon. Then Theotecnus placed the two items, the gospel record, and the Roman sword, on a table before Marinus and demanded him to choose. Marinus looked at the sword, remembering how the hilt felt in his hand, how well he would wield its fine edge. Then he looked at the scroll and remembered all the comfort its words had brought to his soul, all of the precious promises that it contained. He was also reminded of its Christ, who had died cruelly on a tree, then to be raised to life again; a resurrection life that had been imparted to him never to be taken away.

At that moment, it all became clear. The soldier reached forth his hand and took hold of the scroll. With tears in his eyes, Theotecnus said to the soldier, "O my son! Keep that which thou hast chosen, and, despising this present life, hope for the eternal. Depart in good confidence, and receive the crown which the Lord has prepared for thee."

Marinus made his way back to the tribunal. A herald announced his return just as the three hours was winding away. With new confidence and bold demeanor, he stood before the eyes of the tribunal and in the gaze of Judge Achaeus. As the judge opened his mouth to speak, Marinus interrupted, raising his voice so that all could hear: "I have considered the matter, and it was established by the law of the fathers, that God must be obeyed rather than men." Then with great zeal and full assurance, the young man affirmed his faith in Jesus Christ as the one and only true God. The tribunal judge was furious, and immediately called for the execution of Marinus. Moments later, after he was cruelly tortured, Marinus was beheaded and arrived at his chosen destination: the eternal presence of his loving Lord.

It is possible, however unlikely, that we too may be forced to make such a choice under threat of the sword. There are many around the world, for which this old scene, is not a distant possibility, but a very real probability. Their embrace of the faith once delivered to the saints is a costly one. But, in the case of every person on this celestial ball, there is a choice. In closed countries of the Far East or in differing degrees of religious freedom in the west, every person stands at the fork in the road, forced to decide the identity and the authority of the man Jesus Christ. And the path you choose concerning him is the path that, in the end, will indeed make all the difference, for Jesus has said:

If any man will come after me, let him deny himself, and take up his cross, and follow me. For whosoever will save his life shall lose it: and whosoever will lose his life for my sake shall find it.
(Matthew 16:24-25)

THE DEATH OF WILLIAM TYNDALE

The thing that got me was that they scraped his hands. They took a piece of glass or a knife and with the edge, scraped the heel and palm of his hand down to his fingertips. They were trying to remove something, something that they had applied to his hands years ago. It was supposed to be a holy anointing oil. An oil poured on to his hands to signify the sacredness of the duties he would perform. Everything he would touch from the vessels of his service to the bread and the wine he would hand to others, to the anointing the sick and blessing of others, his hands were symbolically anointed of God to perform each sacred task.

But on this mild sixth day of October in 1536, the very men that anointed William's hands were doing everything they could to take it back; to undo what he had done, to use his humiliation and execution as a threat to all who would dare to follow in his steps.

FORGOTTEN

But those anointed hands, grasping pen and ink and feverishly writing line by line, word by word, had already done the work. They had unleashed a fire; removed the blindfold of ignorance to allow in the illumination of the revealed word of God to shine into the hearts and minds of the common man. Scrape all they might, but they would never undo what those anointed hands had already done.

- ෴ -

William Tyndale was born in Gloucestershire, England, around the year 1485. He began a Bachelor of Arts degree at Oxford University in 1506, finishing in 1512 and received his Master of Arts in July 1515. Tyndale was uniquely gifted in the study and used of languages. He became fluent over the years in French, Greek, Hebrew, German, Italian, Latin, and Spanish, as well as his native English. Between 1517 and 1521, he went to the University of Cambridge, also becoming chaplain at the home of Sir John Walsh of Little Sodbury and tutor to his children around 1521.

At the onset of his ministry, he found conflict or instead conflict found him. His opinions and convictions were alarming to his fellow clergymen. Although no formal charges were brought against him, he was brought before church leaders to answer questions concerning some of his statements.

Back in the 14th century, a priest named John Wycliffe had translated the Bible into English. But such work was condemned by the Catholic Church, and a majority of the relatively few handwritten copies were rounded up and destroyed. In 1408, the Church banned all unauthorized translations of the Bible into

THE DEATH OF WILLIAM TYNDALE

English. To ignore this ban would make one guilty of a crime punishable by charges of heresy.

Over one-hundred years later, William Tyndale had a burning desire to translate the Bible into English and voiced this desire openly. The meeting with church officials was contentious, and the clergymen made it clear that no such translation of the scriptures was to be made stating, "We had better be without God's laws than the Pope's." Infuriated at the audacity of such a statement, William boldly said, "I defy the Pope and all his laws; and if God spares my life, ere many years, I will cause the boy that driveth the plow to know more of the Scriptures than thou dost!"

Tyndale left for London in 1523 in hopes of gaining permission to translate the Bible into English from a Bishop Tunstall. Tunstall had worked recently with Erasmus on the compiling of a Greek New Testament, so Tyndale had every reason to suspect that he would be favorable to a translation of the scriptures into English. But Tyndale was refused.

But, a few setbacks would not stifle the determination of this young man. It was plainly evident to him that the will of God was that men of all classes read the word of God. With the help of some British merchants, he set sail for Europe in 1524 to complete the English translation that he had already begun translating. In the town of Cologne in Germany, he found a printer willing to print his English rendering of the New Testament, but midway through the work, reformation opponents caught wind of what he was doing and led a raid on the print shop. Tyndale barely escaped, but not without the few pages that had already been printed.

FORGOTTEN

He secretly made his way to the city of Worms where only a few years past a Catholic Monk took his stand of conscience on the word of God. There William found another printer, and despite some delays and setbacks, by 1526, six-thousand copies of the New Testament were printed and spread all over England and Scotland. Once the Catholic bishops in England found out, they did everything they could to stop the flow of New Testaments into the country; demanding that ships carrying goods over from Europe, be thoroughly searched. Bibles were wrapped in bales of cloth; hidden in barrels of flour. Some even came in individual pages slipped in other larger books to be reassembled in secret upon arrival. The search for these Bibles was so intensive that ships would be forced to endure lengthy inspections before ever entering the docks. Some accounts tell of a drought that took place in 1527 that had crowds awaiting grain from Europe nearly in a riot waiting on these inspections to be completed, putting pressure on church authorities to let down their guard, allowing even more of these Bibles to slip into London.

The Bibles confiscated were burned publicly as an indictment of Tyndale's work. The Archbishop of Canterbury was so desperate to remove the books from circulation that he would pay whatever the cost to buy up all the remaining copies, only to destroy them. Tyndale's friends did just that, charged absorbent rates and delivered the Bibles. The high-profit margin only allowed William to edit and improve his translation and print all the more copies of the New Testament.

Tyndale continued his work on the Old Testament, for which he had to learn Hebrew, a language that he did not know when he arrived in Europe. In 1530 he completed the Pentateuch, the first

THE DEATH OF WILLIAM TYNDALE

five books of the Old Testament, despite having to do the work a second time after his early manuscripts were lost during a shipwreck. At the end of his ministry, 51,000 copies of the New Testament had been distributed in England and Scotland, laying the foundation for reformation in the English speaking world.

Church authorities in England sent many stealthy spies with orders to arrest Tyndale and return him to England to stand trial. But even though he made no significant effort to keep his whereabouts a secret, Tyndale always alluded capture. There is little doubt that a Holy Hand was protecting his way.

When he had accomplished the work that God had set him to do, William Tyndale was captured. A man named Henry Philips posed as a friend interested in the spread of the scriptures. He established a close relationship of trust with Tyndale, even with the protest of Tyndale's trusted inner circle. One night, after having dinner in Phillips home, Tyndale was arrested and taken to the castle of Filford near Brussels. He would remain imprisoned here for the nearly eighteen months, in miserable conditions of sweltering heat and frigid cold, little to no light, ragged clothing and starvation rations; without friends to encourage his heart or books to feed his mind.

The only interaction that he had was with the constant stream of antagonistic priests that continually badgered and baited him, tempting him to recant. But his enduring faith in God which drove him to translate the Bible into English in defiance of Catholic Leadership was unbending in the fires of persecution and imprisonment. He maintained a Christ-like love through to the end. He wrote these words to his accusers: "Christ is the cause why I love thee, why I am ready to do the uttermost of my power for thee, and why I pray for thee. And as long as the cause abideth, so long lasteth the effect; even as it is always day so longs as the sun shineth."

Sometime in the early days of August 1536, he endured the humiliation of being defrocked, stripped of his priestly status in the Catholic Church. In a very public ceremony, he was paraded before a group of presiding bishops wearing his priestly garments (no doubt he was dressed in for this occasion); then forced to kneel. At this point, his hands were scrapped with a knife or a piece of glass in any location where the anointing oil might have touched him renouncing his consecration as a priest. Then the elements of the Lord's Table were placed in his hands and quickly snatched away. Following this, the priestly garments that he wore were torn apart from his body, and the rags of a peasant were placed upon him. He was at that time condemned to death and handed over to secular authorities, so as not to stain the church's hands with the blood of heretics. Having been placed under arrest, he was taken back to the castle of Filford to await execution. A wait that lasted two whole months, probably in hopes of drawing from him a recantation in the face of death. They received no such pleasure.

In the early morning hours of October 6th, William Tyndale was led out of the castle at Filford toward the southern gate where a wooden stake stood in a clearing. The chain that hung from the top of the stake was looped around his neck, then a noose was wrapped around the throat of Tyndale, the end of which threaded through a hole in the stake. His torso and legs were chained to the stake.

THE DEATH OF WILLIAM TYNDALE

As the eyes of all looked upon him, he was given one last opportunity to recant before the presiding panel of bishops and officers. William remained silent. As piles of brushwood and logs were heaped around him, he turned his eyes turned to heaven, and with a distinct cry that could be heard by all, he made his final prayer: "Lord, open the king of England's eyes." With that, the executioner violently pulled on the rope strangling Tyndale in moments. A torch was then applied to the brush, which quickly consumed William Tyndale's body.

Try as they might, they could never undo what the hands of William Tyndale had done. His highly accurate and skillful translation of the scriptures from the ancient Hebrew and Greek manuscripts has had a lasting effect, not only on all subsequent Bible translations but on western civilization as a whole. Studies have shown that 90% of the beloved and highly influential Authorized Version or the King James Version of the Bible was taken directly from Tyndale's translation. Even the Revised Standard Version carries some 75% of Tyndale's work.

This determined and hunted man, hunched over parchments with quill and inkwell, gave the English speaking church such memorable phrases as, "And God said, Let there be light, and there was light"; "Blessed are the poor in spirit: for theirs is the kingdom of heaven."; "Our Father which art in heaven, Hallowed be thy name"; "And God shall wipe away all tears from their eyes." And other phrases, too numerous to name, have become such a part of the English speaking world that newspaper reporters often use such phrases in their headlines without even realizing they are quotations from Tyndale's English translation of the Bible.

FORGOTTEN

Indeed this reveals the sheer genius and linguistic mastery of this servant of God. A mind and heart anointed of God to accomplish a task that no one could stop. For as Tyndale would translate from the words of the Apostle Peter:

...all flesh is as grass, and all the glory of man as the flower of grass. The grass withereth, and the flower falleth away: But the word of the Lord endureth for ever... (1 Peter 1:24-25)

THE GODLY WOMAN OF CHIPPING SODBURY

The term poetic justice is a literary construct used in telling a story. It is usually found at the end of a tale and is defined as the moment in the plot where virtue is ultimately rewarded and vice punished. No matter how many strands of narrative constrain the characters, no matter how far and wide the story may roam, in the end, through some ironic twist of fate, everything turns out as it should. Cinderella becomes a princess. While her evil stepmother and sisters become servants.

However, one does not have to live life very wrong to begin to believe that most of the time poetic justice is only found in fairy tales. Wrongs are seldom made right. Good does not always win in the end. Injustices go unpunished, and the virtuous are rarely praised. The real world is harsh and cruel in its plot and can cause us to doubt that there is such a thing as justice.

FORGOTTEN

Yet justice is written across our conscience. When we see it trampled, there is something within the heart that screams "No! This is wrong." This is the Fingerprint of our Maker. God, the creator, is just. He is the very essence of justice. You see, although we may not see poetic justice played out across the stage of time, in the end, God will make every wrong right. Every man will receive that which his deeds demand at the final judgment.

But there are some instances, where the poetic justice that our hearts seek is not necessarily reserved for some far-off day before the throne of God. Some of them take place right before our eyes. Such was the case with the godly woman of Chipping Sodbury, England.

- ℘)ℭ -

Chipping Sodbury is a small farming village in the southwest of England, founded in the late 12th century by William Crassus the 1st Earl of Albemarle. By the early 16th century, this small community, along with the whole of England, was thoroughly Catholic. It would not be until 1517 that Martin Luther would nail his Ninety-Five Theses to the church house door in Wittenberg, Germany; and even by then, the dawning rays of reformation light would not reach England for years to come.

This does not mean the Catholic Church did not persecute Christian orthodoxy during that period in history. Men like John Wycliffe and William Tyndale, morning stars of the Reformation, had already left their mark on England. The great martyr historian, John Fox, details the persecution and death of such men like William Tylsworth, Thomas Chase, Laurence Ghest, and John

THE GODLY WOMAN OF CHIPPING SODBURY

Browne all in the early years of the 1500s. These men died for the sake of Gospel truth and their condemnation of the idolatry and superstition of the Catholic Church.

Nestled in Foxe's accounts is an obscure story of a nameless woman who was burned at the stake in the town of Chipping Sodbury around this same time during the late years of King Henry VII's reign. Although her name is not given, the account of this woman had a profound impact on the mind of John Foxe who said: "Of all the people who suffered for Christ and His truth, I know of none so admirable as the godly woman put to death in Chipping Sodbury."

There is little known of this woman. Her name is not given. Foxe only addresses her as merely "a godly woman." There is no explicit statement of her charge. The only thing that can be found is that she was charged with heresy. Now, heresy could mean any number of things from suspicion of witchcraft to differing beliefs concerning the sacraments. But when we combine her charge of heresy, with the description of her character as a godly woman, we can rest assured that her accusation is rooted in an unwavering devotion to the truth of God's word.

Foxe's account also sheds light on her tormentor. He is identified as a church chancellor named Dr. Whittington. When mentioned in the context of church matters, a chancellor is a lawyer who represents the church in legal issues. Evidently, Dr. Whittington mercilessly brought serious charges against this godly woman and insisted before Catholic Church leaders that she be not only found guilty but be condemned to death.

FORGOTTEN

As close as can be known, somewhere between 1508 and 1511, this Godly woman was brought before the people of Chipping Sodbury to be executed by being burnt at the stake. There is little doubt that much of the formality surrounding the execution was to elicit a recantation, to cause one to renounce their beliefs under the threat of death. No doubt she was presented to the people of the village, bound to the stake, and a flame kindled at her feet in hopes that she would recant. She could probably see Chancellor Whittington, who was in attendance at the execution, sneer with delight at watching her final moments. But this godly woman refused to allow her fears to cloud her conviction. She held firm to the truth of God's word and committed her dying breaths into the hands of her Lord. Before long, she breathed her last breath in this world, and the flames consumed her mortal shell. The deed being done, the town's people that had gathered to witness the execution, began to disperse to their homes in a quiet uneasiness.

At this exact same moment, on the other side of the village was a butcher going about his daily business. He had to forgo his attendance at the town spectacle because he had a tremendous bull slated for slaughter. As the execution flames further disfigured the lifeless form of this godly woman, the butcher finished securing the beast into position with ropes. He had done this countless times; one sharp blow to the head of the animal should do the trick. The butcher raised his hand and came down with a decisive blow.

But something happened; something that rarely ever happened. The butcher missed and struck a glancing blow to the cow's face. In a panic, the enormous beast lunged backward with all his might; at which the strained ropes that held the animal in place snapped. The suddenly freed bull bolted toward daylight and soon found himself on a city street.

In a frantic crazed gallop, the animal broke into a run. Coming in the opposite direction were crowds of people coming from the execution. One might think this would be a disastrous situation; that this wildly frightened and injured beast would trample people by the dozens. But the most bizarre series of events took place. The direction the bull was running did not lead him away from the commotion and the crowd. No, it took him straight toward it. And even though the bull ran violently toward the people, driving right through the midst of the group, not a single person was hit. That is until it arrived at the town's center, where the execution took place.

It was there that the beast made a straight line, toward one person; seemingly gaining speed, almost as if he were aiming for one individual. And with one powerful thrust, the raging bull rammed his horn into the body of Chancellor Whittington. Eyewitnesses testified to the fact that the bull trotted away with the entrails of Dr. Whittington dangling from its horn.

What took place that fateful day is indeed what we might call poetic justice. And although it does not frequently happen in full view of an on-looking world, it does imprint upon the mind of all who see the biblical truth of the prophet Hosea when he said,

> "...they that sown the wind, and they shall reap the whirlwind."
> (Hosea 8:7)

Or what the Apostle Paul wrote in the Galatian letter:

FORGOTTEN

"Be not deceived; God is not mocked: for whatsoever a man soweth, that shall he also reap." (Galatians 6:7)

Either way, it just goes to show that if you mess with the bull, you get the horns.

WATCHMAN NEE

There is something down in the heart of every human being that whispers the existence of God. Like a shadow that almost makes the perceptible outline of a figure. Some psychologists even suggest that from birth we are hard-wired to believe in God.

I have heard it said many times that there are no atheists in foxholes. Meaning that there are moments in life where, even if we don't intentionally or purposefully believe in God, we will still cry out to Him.

The problem for many is that the response of God is all too silent. They suppose that God's silence is an indication of his absence or is non-existence altogether. They believe that proof of the existence of God would be their ability to summon God at their whim, to stand attention before them, and grant their wish like some genie in a bottle. So when God doesn't respond to their call, they take that as proof that He doesn't exist.

FORGOTTEN

But for those that know their God, those who have not seen yet believe, their confidence is that the God of heaven, is always near; that He is the provider and the sustainer of all things. They possess a belief that no matter how deafening the silence is after their prayer, their Heavenly Father has given His word that He does hear the cry of His children and that He will answer as He sees fit.

Yet there are those times when we as believers long for God to come down and show His power for all to see. We want the equivalent of a high-noon, center of town, in the middle of the street showdown. There are moments when we want the great God of heaven to enter the scene of our world, and like a flash stretch forth His omnipotent Hand to put to naught the evil that threatens us, and doing so right in front of the eyes of a gawking world.

Admittedly that doesn't happen often. For the most part, believers walk by faith and not by sight. However, in the annals of history, there are those times when God does bare His arm and reveal His sovereign authority for all to see. Moments like the account from the life of Chinese Evangelist Watchman Nee in the early 1920s; where God worked in such a wondrous fashion that an entire pagan society was shaken to its core.

- ☙❧ -

Watchman Nee was born on November 4, 1903. Before he was born, Christianity had already made inroads into the towns and villages of China. Nee was born to second-generation Christians. Before he was ever born, he was already dedicated to God. His mother prayed to God that her baby would be a boy, promising "If I have a boy, I will present him to You." Later in his life, Nee's father would remind him saying, "Before you were born, your mother promised to present you to the Lord."

Watchman Nee was a bright and highly intelligent student, often placing in the top of his class. He was ambitious and from all outward indications would have a successful and prosperous career.

However, in 1916, Nee was impressed when his mother came home from a revival meeting and expressed a heartfelt apology to him. In a recent domestic situation, she had unjustly punished him. He was so taken back by the response that he determined to go to the next day's meeting. After coming home from the revival gathering, Nee was deeply affected. Of the experience Nee said, "Previously I had laughed at people who had accepted Jesus, but that evening the experience became real for me, and I wept and confessed my sins, seeking the Lord's forgiveness. As I made my first prayer, I knew joy and peace such as I had never known before."

Nee proved to be a quick learner and grew significantly in the Lord. It wasn't long before Nee was preaching and doing evangelistic outreach. It was during the early 1920s that Watchman Nee suffered a heartbreaking blow. Several brethren with which he had been serving the Lord, informed him that he was no longer welcome to worship with them. At that time, the Chinese government was already placing pressure on Christians to make compromises in their faith. These brethren knew that

FORGOTTEN

Watchman Nee would never do that. They said it would be easier for them to minister without him.

Nee was heartbroken and relocated to more familiar surroundings. Nee tried to move on and continue his work but was deeply depressed. That is when a friend by the name of Faithful Luke came to visit him. In a time of fervent prayer with Faithful Luke, they both sensed that God was saying to them "Leave your problem with Me. You go and preach the Good News!"

Soon after, Faithful Luke received an urgent message from a close friend, asking him to come and preach in the pagan village where she worked as a midwife. It was a small island off the coast of China called Meihwa. These two, Faithful Luke and Watchman Nee took five Christian brothers and began to saturate the island with the gospel. They were zealous and enthusiastic in their gospel endeavors. However, after a week of intense labor, there were no conversions at all. In general, they were just ignored by the town's people.

Kuoching Lee, the youngest member of the group, was frustrated by the disinterest in his words. He shouted out to a crowd of villagers, "What's wrong with you? Why don't you believe?" A voice in the crowd said, "Oh, we do believe. We believe in our great king, Ta-Wang. He never fails us."

When Kuoching questioned the people further about this god, he learned that every year on January 11th they held an elaborate festival to honor Ta-Wang. They took his massive idol from its temple and paraded it through the streets. They feasted and rejoiced and made music and worshiped this idol. They had done this for 286 years, and Ta-Wang had always provided them with beautiful weather on that day. It had not rained on January 11th for 300 years, they boasted.

Kuoching saw his opportunity. He hurriedly shouted, "Then I promise you that our God, who is the true God, will make it rain on the 11th!" The crowd took up his challenge. Say no more," they replied, "If it rains on the 11th then your Jesus is indeed God. We will be ready to hear Him."

Watchman had been preaching in another location when all this took place. So later when he heard this news, he was initially disheartened; and was even tempted to rebuke the young man for being so rash. The 11th was just two days away! However, he stopped himself and took the matter to the Lord in prayer. "Lord, have we taken this too far? Should we leave this village lest your name be maligned?" As he prayed, deep within his heart surfaced the words of 2 Kings 2:14 : "Where is the LORD God of Elijah?"

Watchman was convinced that God would make the skies do what they had not done for three centuries: Rain on January 11th. He was so sure that he took this challenge to the street broadcasting it all over town. The following day would be a showdown between these two deities.

The morning of January 11th was greeted with a cloudless sunrise. Nee watched as villagers went about their day with unusual speed, making preparations for the pagan festivities to come. As Nee went down to meet the others for breakfast, one could feel the tension in the air among the seven evangelists.

FORGOTTEN

Watchman quietly bowed to pray over their morning meal saying, "Father, please accept our prayer as a gentle reminder that you promised to answer the challenge of the demon-god today. Even though not a cloud appears in the sky, we trust in Your promise." And before he could say "Amen" raindrops could be heard striking the roof.

The people of the village, persisted, choosing to ignore the rain. They hurriedly hoisted their large shrine on to its platform and began to carry him down the now slippery streets. As they walked, they could be heard saying, "Ta-Wang, stop this rain and defeat this Jesus." It was about that time that the skies opened up in a torrential downpour. The rain fell so hard and so fast that flash flood ravines began to develop throughout the city. Before long the water reached the level of most porches in the village.

Water rushed down the street where the pagan priests were carrying Ta-Wang and as determined and stubborn as they were to hold up their silent and stiff god, the water was too much. One of the priests slipped and down came Ta-Wang crashing onto the street, breaking its head and left arm. Watchman and his six co-workers laughed with delight and joy! It was a miracle, and God had laid bare His arm and showed Himself strong.

The priests rushed their god into a nearby home for repairs. Later after the rain had stopped, they emerged, with some important news. They proclaimed that the celebration had taken place on the wrong date. It was supposed to be held on the 14th of January at 6 pm, not on the 11th.

WATCHMAN NEE

Watchman Nee knew that this challenge was no match for his God. He prayed confidently: "Lord, give us good weather until that very hour, for there is much to do." For the next three and a half days, Nee's team preached with great boldness on street corners and in marketplaces. More than 30 villagers received the Lord as their Saviour; translated from the darkness of pagan worship into the glorious light of Jesus Christ.

And the weather? It was gorgeous for those days. That is, right up until the 6 o'clock hour of the 14th of January. It was then that another deluge soaked the city of Meihwa. The flood waters of that day broke Ta-Wang's bondage of the people of that island. Scores of people came to know Christ in saving faith. Soon after, an active New Testament Church was born on that island, in that hour.

Nee overcome the consternation and the perplexity in his heart with renewed joy and confidence in God. Nee was strengthened in his faith by this manifestation of God's power. Eventually, that strength of faith in God would give him the grace to spend twenty years of hard labor in a Chinese prison camp.

He was arrested in 1952 because of false charges made by fellow laborers through government coercion. But make no mistake about it, he was imprisoned for his faith in Jesus Christ. Watchman Nee was scheduled to be released in 1967 but was detained in prison until his death on May 30, 1972.

One cannot read the story about what took place on that day with Watchman Nee and his companions without thinking of the account of Elijah on Mount Carmel in the Old Testament book of

FORGOTTEN

1 Kings Chapter 18. Elijah challenged the priests of the pagan god of Baal. A challenge that consisted of two altars made, two sacrifices given, and the god that answered by fire, He is the one true God.

All day the prophets of Baal called and cried out to their god with no response. Then Elijah prayed a sixty-three-word prayer, and fire came from heaven in a flash and consumed the offering and the altar that it rested on.

The God of then, is the God of now! He is unchanged and undiminished in his power. So whether God answers by miraculous power in the public showdowns of our lives or moves and works behind the scenes of circumstance, we are to trust that He is there; and He jealously and tenderly cares for His own.

Elijah made a probing statement to the people witnessing that showdown on top of Mt. Carmel. A statement that ought to echo through the chamber of our hearts and challenge our faith in everyday life:

How long halt ye between two opinions? If the LORD be God, follow him: but if Baal, then follow him. (1 Kings 18:21)

EXTRAS

THE RED RIVER MEETING HOUSE

I remember it was smaller than I thought it would be; and despite the high summer sun, it was dark in the single room cabin. It was hot too, sweltering. That July weekend back in 2005, I had joined several other ministers, along with my pastor, to make a four hour trip to an out of the way one-room log cabin in Kentucky. A log cabin that wasn't even all that old.

It had just been built back in 1994 to be a replica of the original building built somewhere between 1789 and 1792. Some 60 years later, in 1856, that original building simply collapsed in disrepair. Not long after, another building was constructed. But it too eventually had to be torn down due to deterioration and disuse. And for 30 years there was no building at all. Then in 1959, some historically minded people built a log cabin that was supposed to resemble the original structure. But in a mysterious fire, the building burned to the ground in 1992. Then in 1994, an association was formed to raise funds to rebuild once again the historic building, which was completed that same year.

So there I was sitting in a 10-year-old replica of a replica. A building that had been built, in one way or another, four times since the original. But then as we sat on those rough cut timber benches, my pastor reached into his pocket and pulled out a small paperback book. Turning to a particular page, he began to read the account of what took place on those grounds so long ago.

An event that took place out in the middle of nowhere, on the far edge of a fledgling nation, in a region of the country filled with criminals and fugitives. An event, that not only had a profound effect on the local area of Logan County Kentucky, or the frontier state as a whole; but left its mark on succeeding generations in the states of Tennessee, Georgia, Ohio, Virginia, and the Carolinas. And to some degree altered the heart and conscience of America while still laying in the cradle of its infancy.

- ∞)(∝ -

The story of the Red River Meeting House is not confined to the land or the building itself. It's focused on a man; a man by the name of James McGready. He was born in Pennsylvania of Scotch-Irish descent. When he was still a baby, his father moved from Pennsylvania to North Carolina, settling in Guilford County. It was here he spent his childhood.

James was found to be a thoughtful and serious-minded young man. He showed great promise of a kind and honest, manly character. An uncle from Pennsylvania, who was on a visit to his father's family, thought that young James would make an excellent minister and asked James' father and mother if they would allow their son to accompany him to Pennsylvania so that he might get a ministerial education. His parents agreed.

It was during the early days of his education in 1785 that something significant took place in the life of this young man. Under the preaching of a Rev. Mr. Smith, McGready came under great conviction of sin. He realized that his life, no matter how ethical or moral he tried to be, could not bring him acceptance before a Holy God. All of his righteous deeds could not gain him eternal life. James realized that he must be born from above and it wasn't long after that he was soundly saved.

After finishing his education in the fall of 1788, James McGready began to make his way home to North Carolina. On the way home, he passed through Hampden Sidney, Virginia where at that time there was a great move of God in revival throughout the community and particularly at Hampden Sidney College. During his brief stay, McGready spent time with Dr. John Blair Smith, the president of Hampden Sidney College. Dr. Smith was powerfully used of God in connection with a local revival on the college campus. McGready was significantly affected by Smith's influence and by what he witnessed during this time of gracious reviving. It would forever kindle a thirst in his heart for the outpouring of the Spirit of God no matter where the ministry took him.

Upon arriving in North Carolina, he found the local churches dry and dead; barren and lifeless. He attacked the ministry of the word with zeal and fervor. His preaching was a means of awakening during that time, and the fires of local revival began to be fanned. In 1790, Mr. McGready married and became the pastor of a congregation in Orange County. His labor and faithfulness to God started to bring in a great harvest.

But it was not without opposition. McGready was accused of disrupting the lives of hard-working people by all this religious excitement and of creating unnecessary alarm in an otherwise decent and moral people. This opposition went beyond just accusation. On one occasion, the hatred for McGready incited a group of people to overturn the pews of the church and burn his pulpit, and set fire to the building. Even a letter, written in blood was left, threatening harm to him if he did not quit the ministry. This did not deter McGready one bit. He continued his preaching and praying, and over time his dissenters were less and less.

In the late 1790s, Kentucky was a frontier land. It was sparsely populated and many of the folks living there were not looking to be found. Often these frontier lands were places for people to hide from justice back East. One particular area of Kentucky was notorious for such characters. Logan County, KY was known as "Rogue's Harbor" or "Satan's Stronghold." It was overrun with murderers, horse thieves, highway robbers, land speculators and all around con-artists. It was the most dangerous place to live in the nation. Attempts to establish law and order failed time and time again.

Although, we are not sure what was the reasoning behind his decision. Maybe it was a burden to share the gospel of Christ in such a wicked place. Perhaps it was through an invitation to come and help the churches that were struggling in that area. Or maybe it was merely the providential guiding hand of God. But in 1796, James McGready and his family moved to Logan County Kentucky. And by 1797, he had taken the pastoral role in three congregations in Logan County: Gaspar River, Red River, and Muddy River. Although these congregations were small, and interest in spiritual things was anemic, there were some with an earnest desire to follow Jesus Christ. James McGready once again threw everything into the ministry with the same zeal and pursuit of God that he had done in North Carolina. He made significant efforts to arouse the people to their slumbering spiritual condition, as well as making appeals for the conversion of sinners. He also encouraged those that were sincere about the things of God to pray for the outpouring of the Holy Spirit. From 1797 to 1799, McGready preached without any great deal of success. But in the summer of 1799 something changed.

The ministry of James McGready brought with it a long tradition known as the Scottish sacrament season which was still being practiced regularly in Presbyterian congregations. It was an extended time of observing the Lord's Supper over several days, in the warm weather months of the year. It included open-air preaching, large numbers of people often traveling long distances, long vigils of prayer, and was often the scene of dramatic conversions.

In the summer of 1799, a remarkable spirit of prayer was given to these Christians under McGready's care; a sensible heart-felt burden for the dreadful state of sinners outside of Christ. During this protracted meeting for the Lord's Supper, God blessed in a mighty move of His Spirit. The unconverted, under a deep sense of guilt and condemnation, fell from their seats and lay helpless on the floor crying out to God for the saving of their souls. It was such a miraculous week of worship that news of what took place that summer spread all around the countryside. And in the following year, there was a great sense of anticipation for what might happen at the next meeting.

In June of 1800, the Lord's Supper meeting was held at the Red River Meeting House. James McGready was joined by several other ministers for the meeting. These included William Hodge, John Rankin, William McAdow and the brothers John and William McGee, each of whom belonging to different denominations. It was on Monday of the meeting, that while Mr. Hodge was preaching, a woman in the east end of the house got an uncommon blessing. Breaking through the usual order of things, she shouted for some time and then sat down in silence. Soon after the sermon was ended, the people were so wrought upon, that, when they were dismissed, they kept their seats, and wept silently all over the house. Hodge, McGready, and Rankin all quietly made their way out of the building. But the McGee brothers remained inside.

History records what took place next through the eyes of John McGee: "My brother felt such a power come on him that he quit his seat and sat down in the floor of the pulpit. A power which caused me to tremble was upon me. There was a solemn weeping all over the house. Having a wish to preach, I strove against my feelings; at length I rose up and told the people I was appointed to preach, but there was a greater than I preaching and exhorted them to let the Lord God Omnipotent reign in their hearts and to submit to Him and their souls should live. Many broke silence.

THE RED RIVER MEETING HOUSE

The woman in the east end of the house shouted tremendously, I left the pulpit to go to her and as I went along through the people, it was suggested to me, 'You know these people are much for order they will not bear this confusion go back and be quiet.' I turned to go back and was near falling; the power of God was strong upon me I turned again and losing sight of the fear of man I went through the house shouting and exhorting with all possible ecstasy and energy and the floor was soon covered with the slain; their screams for mercy pierced the heavens and mercy came down; some found forgiveness, and many went away from that meeting feeling unutterable agonies of soul for redemption in the blood of Jesus." What followed was a scene of prayer and exhortation that ignited the whole camp.

It is estimated that 500 people came to that Red River meeting. The following month, August 1800, the meeting was held at the Gasper River Church. An estimated 8000 people came to Gasper River and once again God poured out his Spirit. McGready described the miraculous happenings: "The power of God seemed to shake the whole assembly. Towards the close of the sermon, the cries of the distressed arose almost as loud as his voice. After the congregation was dismissed the solemnity increased, till the greater part of the multitude seemed engaged in the most solemn manner. No person seemed to wish to go home–hunger and sleep seemed to affect nobody - eternal things were the vast concern... Persons of every description, white and black, were to be found in every part of the multitude...crying out for mercy in the most extreme distress."

In the following year, 1801, at the Cain Ridge Communion Meeting, there was a staggering 25,000 people gathered in the wilderness, camping in hundreds of wagons. The Second Great Awakening had begun. The revival had transformed the frontier, changing the county from Rogues' Harbor to Souls' Harbor. One man visiting Kentucky in 1802 said, "I have found Kentucky the most moral place I have ever been in. A religious awe seems to pervade the whole country."

Simultaneously, in the northern parts of the United States, God took the hammer of His will and ignited even more sparks of revival by the flint of the Gospel of Jesus Christ. Hundreds of thousands of people were swept into the kingdom of God. These revival fires burned all the way up and into the Civil War. Throughout the regiments of both the North and the South, the saving gospel of Jesus Christ swept soldiers into the safety of God's Hand before their blood was shed on the battlefields of Appomattox, Vicksburg, Chickamauga, and Gettysburg.

As a matter of fact, there is good evidence to suggest that my Great-Great-Great Grand Father, Jeremy Brown, was converted during one of these regimental revivals within the Southern brigades. Coming out of the war safely, he settled in a small town in north Alabama and started a small congregational church that exists to this day.

After he read the account, his voice echoing off the log walls of the rebuilt meeting house, my pastor looked at all us young preachers and said, "Fellas God hasn't changed. The same God that sent revival then is the same One that can send one now! God can change our churches. He can change our communities. He can still change our nation." My pastor then asked all of us to find a little corner in the room, to bow our heads in prayer, and ask God to do it again!

When we see our nation slowly devouring its self, spiraling out of control, we tend to feel powerless; like we can do nothing about it. And, for the most part, we genuinely are powerless. But there is a God in heaven that can, with the outpouring of His Spirit, detour the course of a nation on its way to destruction. God can do it again.

Our hearts must cry out to Him like Psalmist of old:

Wilt thou not revive us again: that thy people may rejoice in thee?
(Psalm 85:6)

IRA SANKEY AND THE CONFEDERATE SOLDIER

Documented stories of near-death experiences go back as far as the 1890s. French psychologists tried to give a term for the accounts of mountain climbers who say they experienced a panoramic review of their life's history during falls that brought them nigh to death. Through the years, reports of those that have been clinically dead and been resuscitated have had some common threads of description that have been classified as stages. At the first stage there is a sense of peace; then there is an out-of-body experience, a feeling of separation from the body. Next, there is a concept of entering into darkness, followed by the sight of an inviting light, then there is the entering into that light. Studies suggest that only 60% experience stage one, whereas only 10% ever recall experiencing the last stage of entering the light.

FORGOTTEN

As you can probably guess, there is a myriad of explanations as to what is taking place in these moments of extreme bodily distress. There are psychological explanations such as depersonalization, dissociation, and fantasy proneness. There are physiological explanations that involve the sudden release of bodily chemicals which affect the temporal lobes of the brain. Then there are spiritual theories that see such experiences as proof of an afterlife and open up to a wide range of cultural and religious explanations.

But not every near-death experience involves a flat line on an EKG. Not every near-death experience contains an out-of-body feeling or an attraction to a welcoming or peaceful light. Most people, at one time or another, have all had such near-death experiences. A childhood bike ride that has a near miss with an oncoming car. The just out of reach fork-lift accident at a job site. The last-second swerve that saved you from a massive and more than likely fatal car crash.

Each of these represents moments in time where we are struck with the reality that we could have been killed, but for whatever reason, we stepped clear at the last moment and were out of harm's way. Most people may attribute this to some latent evolutionary instinct which sparked a sense of danger that caused us to zig instead of zag. But there is an explanation that lies outside of our own ability and intuition; an answer that reveals a God that guides our steps through such places. Sometimes, we can recognize His unseen hand leading us to safety.

But many times we never even realize how near we came to the experience of death. Most of us will never know on this side of

IRA SANKEY AND THE CONFEDERATE SOLDIER

eternity how many times a set of missing car keys and a slight delay in traffic saved our lives. But there is at least one instance in history where on a bright moonlit night, the life of a relatively unknown Union soldier was spared only to find out a decade and a half later, that the Great Shepherd had rescued a His lamb from the jaws of certain death.

- ಸಿಂಜ -

Ira Sankey was born on August 28, 1840, in Edinburg, Pennsylvania to David and Mary Sankey. Being faithful Methodists, they would spend many an evening gathered together singing the old hymns of the faith. Although he had natural musical talent, Ira Sankey's ability to sing came to the forefront during these family gatherings. By the time he was eight years old, he could sing by musical composition. Although he was raised in church all his life, it was not until he was 16 years old that he was converted to Christ during revival meetings at King's Chapel, not too far from his boyhood home.

His newfound faith drove him to serve the Lord with zeal. He labored in the church as a Sunday School Superintendent and teacher, along with leading the church choir. He also at this time, joined his father working at the local bank in his late teenage years.

But it wasn't long after, that the nation was plunged into a Civil War, and Ira was one of the first to answer the call for troops. He enlisted in the Union army shortly after war was declared and was part of a company that was sent to Maryland. Although many a young man's faith has been made shipwreck by the temptations of a soldier's life, Sankey maintained a steady walk with the Lord. He was not only brave as a soldier, but he was zealous for Christ among the other men. His singing ability made him a favorite among his regiment. He organized groups of men to sing and assisted the army chaplain in camp worship services.

After the war, Sankey went back to work with his father, but not at the bank. His father had been appointed by President Lincoln to be a Collector of Internal Revenue. Ira joined his father in this work. But his heart was for serving the Lord through song. As he sang in different meetings and special services, word of his inspiring talent spread. Before long he was receiving invitations to sing all over western Pennsylvania and eastern Ohio. He could be found singing at denominational conventions, Bible conferences, and political rallies. He was gone so much that his father was quoted as saying, "I'm afraid Ira will never amount to anything. All he does is run around the country with a hymn-book under his arm!" Ira's quick-witted mother shot back, "Well, I'd rather see him with a hymn-book under his arm, than with a whiskey bottle in his pocket!"

In June of 1870, Sankey went to Indianapolis, Indiana for an international convention for which he had been appointed a delegate. He was anxious and excited about the trip for he had learned that renown Evangelist D.L. Moody would be there. He had heard and read much about the work of Moody in Chicago and was looking forward to hearing him preach.

He arrived at the service a little late that morning but found a seat next to a Presbyterian minister that he knew. History suggests that the singing during the early morning meeting was dull and

IRA SANKEY AND THE CONFEDERATE SOLDIER

spiritless. The Presbyterian minister beside Sankey encouraged him to stand and sing at the next opportunity. As Mr. Moody requested a song, Sankey rose and sang the song "There Is a Fountain Filled with Blood." He did it with such heartfelt emotion that it wasn't long before the building rang with the voices of all present. The meeting took on a whole new energy as God worked in the hearts of many.

Following the meeting, Sankey was formally introduced to Moody who instantly began to ask straightforward questions about his family and career. Sankey had married not long after the war, and he and Fanny had one child by then. He told Moody that he was working in the government at that time. Moody remarked, "You'll have to give it up!" "Why?" Sankey replied, a little surprised at the remark. "To come help me in my work at Chicago." Sankey said, "I can't leave my business." Moody responded, "You must: I have been looking for you for the last eight years."

Although Ira was very hesitant about such a significant decision, Moody invited him to meet him on a particular street corner the following day. When Sankey arrived, Moody pointed to a large wooden crate, asking him to stand up there and sing something. Sankey complied and sang the hymn "Am I a Soldier of the Cross." People from everywhere within earshot stopped what they were doing to gather around to hear Sankey sing.

Following the song, Moody took his turn on the box and began to address the large crowd that had gathered to hear Sankey's singing. Moody preached, and the people hung on his every word. Even in such a spontaneous event, it was clear that something special had been discovered. Although it would be another six months before Sankey would give in to Moody's request, a lasting bond of friendship and a spirit of partnership in the work of God was formed that day. A relationship that God would use to powerfully impact the world.

Later that year, at 30 years of age, Sankey began to work with D.L. Moody in Chicago. Sankey had not been working long with Moody when the great fire raged through the city of Chicago in October of 1871. Sankey narrowly escaped danger to his own life during this tragedy. Although Moody and his family were saved, he lost practically everything. By the following year, Sankey had moved his whole family to Chicago to help Moody rebuild.

They also began evangelistic campaigns in various cities as their partnership grew even stronger. At the events, the plain-spoken Moody would arrest the attention of his hearers with the compelling words of gospel truth. Then Sankey would conclude the appeal for sinners to come to Christ with songs of earnest emotion. And people would respond to the gospel, believing on Jesus Christ, night, after night, after night.

In 1873, Moody and Sankey along with their families traveled to the British Isles to begin a series of meetings for which they had been invited by two well-known pastors. Upon their arrival, it seemed as though the campaign was to end before it ever started. The two pastors had died; there were no scheduled meetings. Although Moody had preached in England before, he was not widely known. Remembering a standing invitation in York to come and speak if he ever returned to England, Moody made arrangements for evangelistic services to begin there. Even

IRA SANKEY AND THE CONFEDERATE SOLDIER

though as few as 50 people went to the first service, attendance quickly escalated when a leading Baptist minister of the city, F.B. Meyer, gave his hearty endorsement to the meeting. From there, invitations began to come in from all over the country.

D.L. Moody and Ira Sankey spent the next two years in evangelistic campaigns all over Britain, Scotland, and Ireland. Thousands were converted to Jesus Christ during these years. A spirit of revival swept over city after city, igniting churches, and changing communities. It has been said that, through Moody and Sankey, God "gave Britain perhaps the greatest spiritual movement since the days of George Whitfield and John Wesley."

Indeed it was England, not America, which discovered the evangelistic team of Moody and Sankey. By the time they returned to the U.S. in 1875, D.L. Moody and Ira Sankey were household names. They took the North American continent by storm, holding meetings all over the United States, Canada, and Mexico. The impact of their ministry has left an indelible mark that is still seen to this day. Their evangelistic work continued well into the late 1890s. It is unclear just how many lives were changed by God's usage of these two men. If one were to include the lasting legacy of their writings, songs, and educational institutions, their impact could well be in the millions of souls added to the Kingdom of God.

There is little doubt that what we know of D.L. Moody and God's use of him is due in large part to the musical contribution of Ira Sankey. In fact, D.L. Moody was once asked about the importance that a gospel singer and song leader such as Ira Sankey brought to his meetings. Moody responded. "If we can only get people to have the words of the Love of God coming from their mouths, it's well on its way to residing in their hearts."

But all that God had accomplished through these men might not have been. All the millions of people that gathered to hear the words that they would sing and speak might not have come. All of the souls that were saved, all of the lives that were changed, all of the families that were put back together might have remained lost, wayward, and broken. All of the educational institutions and soul-stirring songs might not have been born had things gone differently on one very critical night.

On Christmas Eve 1876, Ira Sankey was taking a steamboat up the Delaware River. Once again his fame and notoriety had preceded him. And while he was on deck, several people recognized him and asked him to sing a song for them. Sankey wanted to oblige and took a moment to think of a song. In his mind, he thought of singing a Christmas song. But a familiar melody rose to the surface of his heart, a song that he had sung so many times yet its enduring truth was such a comfort to his heart. His deep baritone voice sounded strong over the hum of the steam engines: "Savior, like a shepherd, lead us, much we need thy tender care; in thy pleasant pastures feed us, for our use thy folds prepare. Blessed Jesus, blessed Jesus! Thou hast bought us, thine we are. Blessed Jesus, blessed Jesus! Thou hast bought us, thine we are."

The satisfied crowd clapped with light applause and smiles of gratitude as Sankey finished the final chorus. When the crowd began to disburse, a man emerged from the group and introduced himself to Sankey. As they stood and exchanged pleasantries, Ira took note of the man's southern accent. The stranger asked him if

IRA SANKEY AND THE CONFEDERATE SOLDIER

he ever served in the Union Army. "Yes, as a matter of fact, I did; I enlisted in the spring of 1860." Then the man asked a rather peculiar question: "Do you remember doing picket duty on a bright moonlit night in 1862 while singing the very same song you just sang?" Rather uneased by the question, Ira replied "Yes, I do. Were you there too...?" The man slowly shook his head yes and then began to tell his story.

Yes, he was there, out in the woods near a Union Army encampment just outside of Sharpsburg, Maryland. He was watching the soldiers that night from a grove of trees just across the creek. As a Confederate sniper, he was looking for that right opportunity to take out a Union soldier. He waited until twilight, depending on a bright full moon to light his target. Finally, an evening sentry came out to stand guard. He decided that this poor soul would be his target.

He rested his rifle against an oak tree as he waited for the right moment. After a while, the guard came into full view of his rifle's sites. He pulled the hammer of the rifle back slowly and put the soldier in his sights. With a deep breath, he let out a slow and calming exhale. His pulse slowed, his focus sharpened. His finger rested on the cooled trigger, as he added more and more pressure.

It was at that precise moment, that sentry did something surprising. Out of the blue, he raised his eyes toward heaven and began to sing. His rich, deep voice filled the valley with the words, "Savior, like a shepherd lead us, much we need thy tender care…" The sniper suddenly stopped. Relaxing from his tense concentrated stance, he thought, "I'll just let him finish singing. He's mine anyways. I can't miss from this distance."

FORGOTTEN

But the more he listened, the more he thought of his beloved Christian mother. She used to sing that very same song in his boyhood home. She had died some years back, and the song brought a flood of memories to his heart. By the time the guard finished the last stanza, the sharpshooter's eyes were filled with tears, it was useless to aim at the Yankee soldier now. The emotional Confederate simply lowered his rifle, turned, and quietly walked back to his regiment that night.

The stranger told Sankey when he sang that song tonight, he knew without a doubt that this was the voice of the man that he could not shoot on that night so long ago. The man began to heave with tears and to pour out his heart concerning his wayward life after the war. He then pleaded with Sankey to lead him to this Shepherd he was singing about. Sankey put his arm around his former enemy, an enemy that was a hairs breath away from ending Ira's life, and shared with him the wondrous story of God's redeeming love. And in that hour, they both worshipped the Great Shepherd that led them safely into the fold.

That night, Ira Sankey received a precious Christmas gift: The gift of seeing first hand in his life, what no doubt happens on countless occasions in the life of every single individual on this planet at one time or another. The gift of tracing God's hand of care and protection through a world teeming with unseen and unrealized dangers; the gift of realizing there is indeed a God who knows what dangers lurk around every twist and bend of life and is able to rescue us from the very teeth of evil.

The second stanza of Ira Sankey's fateful song that night reads, "We are thine, thou dost befriend us, be the guardian of our

IRA SANKEY AND THE CONFEDERATE SOLDIER

way…" For those who have received and believed upon the Good Shepherd, the shepherd that gives his life for the sheep, Jesus Christ, we can say He is the guardian of our way; we can agree, with the words of David, the shepherd boy who one day became king,

The Lord is my Shepherd, I shall not want. (Psalm 23:1)

EPILOGUE

FORGOTTEN

THE GOSPEL

Each of the historical accounts in the previous chapters relays the story of an individual that has experienced the life-changing power of the gospel of Jesus Christ or has willingly entered into death for the sake of that gospel. In each case, it is the gospel story of Jesus and the importance of that story which led them to live such extraordinary lives.

The truth of that gospel starts with the fact that death is sure. Ten out of ten people die. It's sad but true -- no matter what you do, you will die. The reason for death is that you have sinned against God. Let's see if that's true:

Have you ever lied (even once)? Ever stolen (anything)? Jesus said, *"...whosoever looketh on a woman to lust after her hath committed adultery with her already in his heart." (Matthew 5:28)* Ever looked with lust?

If you have said "Yes" to these three questions, by your own admission, you are a lying, thieving, adulterer at heart; and we've only looked at three of the Ten Commandments (Exodus 20). How will you do on Judgment Day? Will you be innocent or guilty? You know that you will be guilty, and end up in Hell. However, that is not God's will. God takes no pleasure in the death of the wicked. He is not willing that any should perish, but all have eternal life.

For this reason, God has provided a way for you to be forgiven. He sent His Son Jesus to take the punishment for your law-breaking.

> *But God commendeth his love toward us, in that, while we were yet sinners, Christ died for us. (Romans 5:8)*

God showed how much he loved you by sending Jesus to die in your place on the cross.

After Jesus died, he was buried in a borrowed tomb, putting away our sin for us. Then the miracle of all miracles took place. Jesus was raised from the grave alive, defeating death forever. He was seen by many who were then willing to die for the truth of Jesus' resurrection. When Jesus rose from the grave, he proved that he is the only one to save us from sin.

So now *"God…commandeth all men everywhere to repent (turn, change direction)…" (Acts 17:31)* and to *"Believe on the Lord Jesus Christ, and thou shalt be saved…"(Acts 16:31)* God demands that we make a U-Turn on the road of life. He requires that we stop living in rebellion from Him and entrust our lives to Him.

THE GOSPEL

You can repent by calling out to the Lord.

...whosoever shall call upon the name of the Lord shall be saved."
(Romans 10:13)

You can do this by telling the Lord you are sorry for your sins (name them); that you believe Jesus died on the cross to forgive your sins; and you trust Him with your life.

The Bible says *"Therefore if any man be in Christ, he is a new creature...."* (2 Corinthians 5:17) Being a child of God means you have a new life, new heart, and new desires. Find a Bible-believing church to worship Jesus and serve Him in love. Read the Bible daily and obey what you read. God will never let you down.

SOURCES

The following books websites have been beneficial in formulating these small biographical sketches of characters that have (for the most part) passed out of current collective memory. I am indebted to these authors' excellent works and highly recommend them. Many of these were the point of origin that sparked my interest in knowing more about these characters. Other information has come from general references and public domain sources.

JERRY MCAULEY
More Real Stories ©2000 by Robert J. Morgan (Thomas Nelson Publishers)

TRANSFORMED or The History of a River Thief ©1876 by Jeremiah McAuley

Image Attribution: McAuley, Jeremiah. Transformed or The History of a River Thief. Self-Published, 1876

MEL TROTTER
Mel Trotter - A Biography ©2015 by Fred C. Zarfas

Image Attribution: Mel Trotter Ministires
https://www.meltrotter.org/themission/history

ANDRES OF THE MUINANE TRIBE
Sent To The River God Forgot ©1995 by Jim & Janice Walton (Tyndale House Publishers)

FORGOTTEN

Real Stories ©2000 by Robert J. Morgan (Thomas Nelson Publishers)

Image Attribution: Sent to the River God Forgot ©1995 by Jim & Janice Walton (Tyndale House Publishers)

GENESIUS OF ROME
Blessed Among Us: Day by Day with Saintly Witnesses ©2016 by Robert Ellsberg (Give Us This Day Publishers)

The Lives of the Fathers, Martyrs, and Other Principal Saints: Compiled from Original Monuments and Other Authentic Records, Illustrated with the Remarks of Judicious Modern Critics and Historians, Volume 8 ©1815 by Alban Butler

Image Attribution: Catholic Online; https://www.catholic.org/saints/saint.php?saint_id=185

STUART HAMBLEN
Then Sings My Soul - ©2003 by Robert J. Morgan (Thomas Nelson Publishers)

Stuart Hamblen
https://en.wikipedia.org/wiki/Stuart_Hamblen/. Accessed 30 January 2017

Image Attribution: Hamblen Music Company; http://www.hamblenmusic.com/home/stuart-hamblen/photo-gallery/1908-1948#prettyPhoto[gal]/2/

SOURCES

CHARLOTTE ELLIOTT
A Treasury of Hymn Stories ©1945 by Amos R. Wells
Then Sings My Soul - ©2003 by Robert J. Morgan (Thomas Nelson Publishers)

Charlotte Elliott
https://en.wikipedia.org/wiki/Charlotte_Elliott Accessed 9 October 2017

Image Attribution: Sutherland, Allan. Famous Hymns of the World, Their Origin and Their Romance. New York, Frederick A. Stokes Company, 1906

THE BIBLE ON THE BOUNTY
Real Stories ©2000 by Robert J. Morgan (Thomas Nelson Publishers)

HMS Bounty https://en.wikipedia.org/wiki/HMS_Bounty Accessed 11 March 2017

Image Attribution: By Dan Kasberger [CC BY-SA 3.0 (https://creativecommons.org/licenses/by-sa/3.0)], from Wikimedia Commons

THE KING OF CHATTANOOGA
50 Years on the Battle Front with Christ: A Biography of Mordecai F. Ham ©2005 (Reprint) by Edward E. Ham (Larry Harrison Publishing)

Prohibition in the United States
https://en.wikipedia.org/wiki/Prohibition_in_the_United_States Accessed 12 February 2017

FORGOTTEN

Image Attribution: Tennessee State Library and Archives; https://tnsos.org/tsla/imagesearch/images/15985.jpg

WILLIAM HUNTER
Foxe's Christian Martyrs of the World ©1989 by John Foxe (Barbour Publishing)

William Hunter (martyr)
https://en.wikipedia.org/wiki/William_Hunter_(martyr)
Accessed 20 June 2016

Image Attribution: The Acts and Monuments by John Foxe; Published in 1563; Woodcut Image

JOHN BROWN OF PRIESTHILL
John Brown (Covenanter)
https://en.wikipedia.org/wiki/John_Brown_(Covenanter)
Accessed 17 January 2017

The History of John Brown of Priesthill
https://drmarkjardine.wordpress.com/2014/04/20/the-history-of-john-brown-of-priesthill/ by Dr. Mark Jardine
Accessed 17 January 2017

A Cloud of Witnesses for the Royal Prerogatives of Jesus Christ; being the last speeches and testimonies of those who have suffered for the truth in Scotland, since the year 1680 ed. J. H. Thomson (Edinburgh and London, 1871? [1714])

Six saints of the Covenant; Peden: Semple: Welwood: Cameron: Cargill: Smith by Patrick Walker, 1666?-1745?; David Hay Fleming, 1849-1931

SOURCES

Image Attribution: Sketches of the Covenanters, by J.C. Mcfeeters, 1913

DR. ROWLAND TAYLOR
Foxe's Christian Martyrs of the World ©1989 by John Foxe (Barbour Publishing)

Rowland Taylor
https://en.wikipedia.org/wiki/Rowland_Taylor Accessed 19 August 2016

Image Attribution: The Acts and Monuments by John Foxe; Published in 1563; Woodcut Image

MARGARET WILSON
Article by ABC NEWS on abcnews.go.com entitled "Opposite of Loneliness" by Marina Keegan; Accessed May 30, 2012

Margaret Wilson (Scottish martyr)
https://en.wikipedia.org/wiki/Margaret_Wilson_(Scottish_martyr) Accessed 30 September 2016

Image Attribution: John Everett Millais [Public domain], via Wikimedia Commons

JAMES ABBES
Foxe's Christian Martyrs of the World ©1989 by John Foxe (Barbour Publishing)

James Abbes Burned in Bury, England by Dan Graves, https://www.christianity.com/church/church-

FORGOTTEN

history/timeline/1501-1600/james-abbes-burned-in-bury-england-11629988.html Accessed 20 October 2016

Image Attribution: The Acts and Monuments by John Foxe; Published in 1563; Woodcut Image

MAEYKEN WENS
The Bloody Theater; or Martyrs Mirror of the Defenseless Christians, Published in 1660 by Thieleman J. Van Braght; translated into English by Joseph F. Sohm (Public Domain)

Image Attribution: The Bloody Theater; or Martyrs Mirror of the Defenseless Christians by Thieleman J. Van Braght

MARINUS OF CAESAREA
The Works of Eusebius Pamphilius: Church History, Life of Constantine, Oration in Praise of Constantine; Chapter XV. — The Martyrdom of Marinus at Cæsarea
https://www.ccel.org/ccel/schaff/npnf201.iii.xii.xvi.html Accessed 2 March 2017

Marinus of Caesarea
https://en.wikipedia.org/wiki/Marinus_of_Caesarea Accessed 2 March 2017

Image Attribution: By Alfvan Beem [CC0], from Wikimedia Commons

THE DEATH OF WILLIAM TYNDALE
Foxe's Christian Martyrs of the World ©1989 by John Foxe (Barbour Publishing)

SOURCES

William Tyndale
https://en.wikipedia.org/wiki/William_Tyndale Accessed 18 July 2017

The Daring Mission of William Tyndale ©2015 by Steven J. Lawson (Reformation Trust)

Image Attribution: The Acts and Monuments by John Foxe; Published in 1563; Woodcut Image

THE GODLY WOMAN OF CHIPPING SODBURY
Foxe's Christian Martyrs of the World ©1989 by John Foxe (Barbour Publishing)

Image Attribution: The Acts and Monuments by John Foxe; Published in 1563; Woodcut Image

WATCHMAN NEE
More Real Stories ©2000 by Robert J. Morgan (Thomas Nelson Publishers)

Watchman Nee: Sufferer for China ©1998 by Bob Laurent (Barbour Publishing)

Watchman Nee https://en.wikipedia.org/wiki/Watchman_Nee Accessed 29 July 2016

Image Attribution: By Unknown author [Public domain], via Wikimedia Commons

THE REDRIVER MEETING HOUSE
A History of Kentucky Baptists 1885 by J. H. Spencer

FORGOTTEN

History of the Red River Meeting House
http://www.rrmh.org/history Accessed 22 July 2016

James McGready: Son of Thunder, Father of the Great Revival by John Thomas Scott
http://www.cumberland.org/hfcpc/McGreJTS.htm Accessed 22 July 2016

James McGready Presbyterian Minister 1763-1817
http://www.cumberland.org/hfcpc/McGready.htm Accessed 22 July 2016

James McGready 1763-1815
http://www.therestorationmovement.com/_states/kentucky/mcgready.htm Accessed 22 July 2016

Red River Meeting House
https://en.wikipedia.org/wiki/Red_River_Meeting_House Accessed 22 July 2016

The Beginning Days of the Second Great Awakening; "It happened in Kentucky" by Jonathan Pollard
https://jonathanpollard.wordpress.com/2013/03/05/the-beginning-days-of-the-second-great-awakening-it-happened-in-kentucky/ Accessed 22 July 2016

Image Attribution: By Crystal Chapman [GFDL (http://www.gnu.org/copyleft/fdl.html) or CC BY-SA 3.0 (https://creativecommons.org/licenses/by-sa/3.0)], via Wikimedia Commons

SOURCES

IRA SANKEY AND THE CONFEDERATE SOLDIER
Near-death Experience https://en.wikipedia.org/wiki/Near-death_experience Accessed 7 December 2016

Guide's Greatest Change of Heart Stories ©2012 by Rich Edison (Review and Herald Publishing Association)

The American Evangelists, Dwight L. Moody and Ira D. San Key, With An Account Of Their Work In England And America ©1877 by Elias Nason D. Lothrop & Co. Publishers

Image Attribution: By Davis Garber [Public domain], via Wikimedia Commons

GOSPEL
Silhouette of Cross Under Cloudy Sky Photo by Aaron Burden on Unsplash

COVER
Created by modifying "Ominous" [https://www.flickr.com/photos/ankakay/4101391453] (© Ankakay [https://www.flickr.com/photos/ankakay/] (Licensed under CC BY 4.0))

To order your copy, go to:
http://forgottenpodcast.com/servants-missionaries

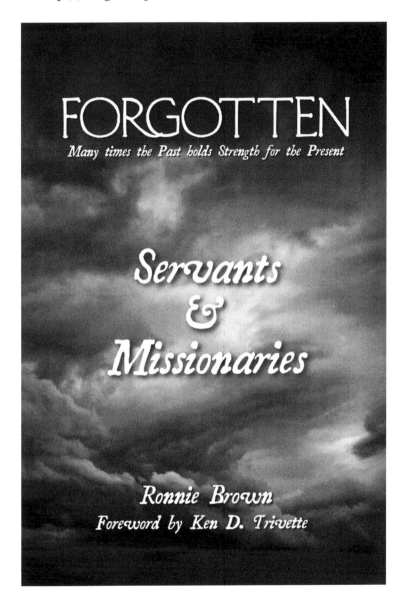

To listen to more stories like these, be sure to go to:
www.forgottenpodcast.com

What people are saying about the Forgotten Podcast:

★ ★ ★ ★ ★ - "If you are a Christian preacher, or anyone who loves the Lord, you need to subscribe to this podcast. Ronnie's scripts are well written, heart-warming, faith stirring, and thoroughly researched." - Bobby Bosler, Professor at Baptist College of Ministry

★ ★ ★ ★ ★ - "Brother Ronnie is bringing history to life with these awesome stories. I really appreciate his heart for this and how professional it is produced. Great job brother!" - Travis Sharpe, Founder/President of Unsheltered International

★ ★ ★ ★ ★ - "What a strength can be found in remembering what God has done in the past...As we have listened, we have chuckled, shed tears, been encouraged and felt conviction. The stories have challenged us and stirred our hearts." - Brian Andrews, Pastor of Amazing Grace Baptist Church

★ ★ ★ ★ ★ - "The most riveting and sobering podcast I have ever heard. I invite you, no...I implore you to listen along with me on this audio journey." - Steven Craig Policastro Jr., Founder/Executive Vice-President of the International Association for Creation